WHERE DO YOU FIT IN?

DEFINE YOUR ESSENTIAL GIFTS & MAKE SOME NOISE

WHERE DO YOU FIT IN?
DEFINE YOUR ESSENTIAL GIFTS & MAKE SOME NOISE

DIANNE A. ALLEN, MA

Copyright © 2019 Dianne A. Allen, MA

All rights reserved. No part of this book may be reproduced by any mechanical, photographic or electronic process, or in the form of a phonographic recording; nor may it be stored in a retrieval system, transmitted or otherwise copied for public or private use – other than for "fair use" as brief quotation embodied in articles and reviews – without prior written permission by the author.

The author of this book does not dispense medical advice or prescribe the use of any technique as a form of treatment for physical, emotional or medical problems without the advice of a physician, either directly or indirectly. The intent of the author is only to offer information of a general nature to help you in your quest for emotional and spiritual well-being. In the event you use any of the information in this book for yourself, which is your constitutional right, the author and the publisher assume no responsibility for your actions.

Because of the dynamic nature of the internet, any web addresses or links contained in this book may have changed since publication and may no longer be valid. Any people depicted herein are fiction and are not representing any specific person.

Cover design by Shake Creative, Tampa, FL
Interior design by Richard Jibaja
Edited by James McAdams
ISBN-13: 978-0-9995778-4-4
Library of Congress Control Number: 2019917365
Printed in USA

For
Jamie Manning

And now here is my secret, a very simple secret: It is only with the heart that one can see rightly; what is essential is invisible to the eye.

Le Petit Prince (1943)

TABLE OF CONTENTS

Acknowledgments		08
A Message from Dianne		09
Foreword		11
Introduction		13
Chapter 1	Where Do You Fit in Anyway?	16
Chapter 2	The Creators	23
Chapter 3	The Workers	27
Chapter 4	The Weavers	30
Chapter 5	The Harmonizers	34
Chapter 6	The Ballers	38
Chapter 7	The Development of an Essential	41
Chapter 8	Things to Consider for Each Essential Variation	45
Chapter 9	Your Role and Relationship with the Universal Source	57
Chapter 10	Your Expansion and Transformation	67
Chapter 11	Faith in Action	73
Chapter 12	Health Challenges Caused by Avoidance and Denial	83
Chapter 13	You Are Not Alone	97
Chapter 14	Making Noise as an Essential in the Modern World	114
Chapter 15	Action Steps to Bring Your Essential Gifts into Daily Life	126
Appendix I	An Unsuspecting Essential Comes of Age	129
Appendix II	Morning and Evening Affirmations	132
Summary	A Never Ending Invitation	133
About the Author, Dianne A. Allen, MA		136

Acknowledgments

I would like to acknowledge all the courageous souls who are transforming and awakening. This was written for you as you move along your path. For all those who have gone before and those who are the torchbearers, I commend you and your work with deep gratitude and respect.

Thank you, Susan Biszewski, for your listening ear and inspired conversations. You are an Essential! Thank you for writing the foreword for this book and being supportive of this work.

Walter and Cheryl Manning are Jamie's parents. This book is dedicated to Jamie as he is a young essential, sharing his magnificent gifts with the world. Walter and Cheryl are loving, kind and present parents. Knowing this family and spending time with them warms my heart and inspires me for our future. Thank you for trusting me.

Thank you to those who support my work and my journey. When the road is challenging, your words of encouragement and your listening ears are the magic that fans the flames of my inner fire!

I acknowledge and thank you, my reader, for following your vision and allowing your Essential gifts to emerge.

To all the clients and retreat participants over the past years, I thank you for your participation in the unfolding of my own Essential gifts as I make noise. Join me, won't you?

A Message from Dianne

You are essential. You are important in the little and the grand parts of life. You may not feel like you fit in, yet you fit in perfectly. Some of the most wonderful people are the ones who don't fit into boxes created by others. We are all like pieces of a puzzle, meant to fit in the perfect place. Our mission is to *feel* our way into this perfect place and thrive.

When you are thriving, the entire world benefits. When you are shut down or merely existing, everything slows down and is muted on levels you cannot yet see or understand.

Your mission is to uncover your unique gifts and their variations. Your vision is meant for you to accomplish or it would not be in your mind and heart. You are an Essential.

The *Where Do You Fit In?* manual is designed to present you with the variations of essential gifts that set you apart as a vital human being on this planet. You may find yourself in more than one place, for many Essentials are blends of variations.

You are on the path to discovery, attunement, and unfoldment. Truly your life is being enriched deeply by your decision to let your gifts surface and make your noise! Discover how to live more fully with purpose and determination by living in the present, breathing, allowing your unique gifts to emerge and illuminate the world. Speak words that align with your Vision and enriches the lives of those around you.

Behold the Divine beauty in yourself and others. See the sacred in the everyday events, people, and interactions. Allow your smile to radiate, touching the hearts of those who are searching or seeking. Embrace your personal journey as well as the path of others with your beautiful inner radiance.

Plant your spiritual garden with seeds of kindness, compassion, gratitude, love, and self-care. Allow yourself to receive the nourishment of these things from your garden and the gardens of others.

Create a daily practice that fosters transformation and progress along your path of discovery and awakening. It is in being generous that you are transformed. Because there are so many varied ways to language the topics of transformation and spirituality, I have chosen in this book to interchange language from diverse worldviews. I invite you to release any resistance or judgment and replace your own words for the concepts if you wish. It is the overarching ideas that are most important.

You will notice that I use Essential as a noun in much of this book. This is a new way to describe you and your unique gifts.

Welcome. I am glad you are here.

Foreword

To say that Dianne A. Allen understands or "totally gets" the *nature* of human nature falls very short in describing the impact of her influence in transforming individuals with whom she has encountered over the years. Her reputation proceeded her in my community and in the ever-growing realm of social media as she continued to pop up in my Facebook feed. Our friendship began with her giving me one of her books, *The Loneliness Cure*, to review for a ministry that I was developing in my parish. By the time I reached page 21, I had highlighted in several colors, noted in 40% of the margins, and written in an old journal, something may I add, that I had not done in years. She had, simply, concisely, and in laypersons terms, provided me with a root cause analysis of human pain and suffering. After finishing reading the book, I contacted her to meet for dinner to discuss several of her points. Dianne did not disappoint. Her wisdom, joy, generous spirit and ability to see right through to the heart of a person reminds me of a happy camper moving comfortably and intuitively through the gloomy night with a big ole flashlight.

Over several dinners our dialogue evolved, and our discussions turned to the concept of individuals who are intuitive, who make connections, who think differently, who see pieces and parts and colors and shapes that most people do not necessarily see. Individuals encouraged to listen to their own intuition will find confidence and migrate toward optimism, resilience, hope and spiritual transformation. Once transformed, people will move beyond the ordinary to pure essence, the habitual "being." They will become the fountain of optimism, the example of resilience and the well-spring of hope. Through the process, these individuals spiritually transform and, in turn, have the capability of spiritually transforming others.

The benefit, of course, to the larger picture of life and humanity is that they become the catalysts of hope and courage that offsets the inhibitors of joy and contributors of fear. But being the catalyst does not always result in an easy path. I have read about individuals who capture this essence, who were the catalyst, who grew in their spirituality and found grace – but they also struggled to find that place where they fit in. They are the saints and quiet unknown individuals who when the moment arose, made some noise, made things happen and became remarkable heroes – some remain unknown and others like Joan of Arc, Nelson Mandela, Oskar Schindler have a place in our history books.

In a time of conflicting priorities, of doubt and fear, Dianne does it again by shifting the paradigm away from helplessness and hopelessness, and resurrecting language of essence and spiritual being in her new book *Where Do You Fit In*? She does this by shining the flashlight in the dark corners and inviting us into the light of spiritually "be" coming. Dianne creates a synergy between the thing and the action, the noun and the verb. And she calls those individuals the **Essentials**. The **Essentials** are those people who tap into their essence, develop their spirituality, strive to exceed their potential and find their place to "be" in the world. They are the saints in training, the quiet and restless ones who she will coach to make noise and find their own flashlights. Thus, making the world a much better place, if not lighter place.

Susan Biszewski, MA

Apprenticeship Coordinator
Department of Labor
Florida Apprenticeship Program

Introduction

> *See the light in others and treat them as if that is all you see.*
> *~~Dr. Wayne Dyer*

Most likely you are feeling some sort of change happening within and around you. There are no real words to describe how you are feeling. You may be having dreams that you don't understand or find yourself seeing life and yourself differently than before. Our world is changing. You are part of the change if you wish to be. On these pages, you will find inspiration, information and the invitation to continue your path of transformation with a clear focus.

All these changes are part of the awakening and potential transcendence of an Essential. An Essential is someone who has a deeper mission and calling to be of benefit to the larger community. You know you are an Essential when you have a relentless inner push to grow and expand that sometimes creates conflict with your old paradigms and rules for engaging your world. An Essential experiences life from this sublime perspective and is intimately connected to Earth, all sentient beings, and the greater meaning of this powerful journey we call *life*. Your Essential nature affords you the opportunity to grow and expand in ways that are profound and maybe even out of your current understanding. This is exciting.

I use the term Essential to describe a way of being in the world rather than a new-age type of reference. Essentials are naturally drawn to existential questions. I hear many Essentials speaking of transcendent ideas and experiences. The mission and responsibility of an Essential is meaningful and should be taken seriously. Many Essentials are creating innovative changes that move humanity forward toward a more unified consciousness. Your essential gift is meant to emerge and make some noise. The noise you will make will be your individual, unique expression of your Essential variation. Only you can bring this gift to the world.

There is a time and place to bring your knowledge, gifts, and awareness to the table. Essentials are born into this path and calling, whether you know it or not. (See my story in Appendix I) Your Essential experience is qualitatively different than others who may have similar interests yet are not journeying in the same manner. In many ways, as an Essential, you are a spiritual warrior, a visionary. Compare the experience of watching a movie in black and white with mono sound to 3D High Definition color with surround sound. It may be the same movie, yet your experience of the movie is qualitatively different. The black and white movie or life experience may be fun or entertaining, yet the depth may not be present due to the restrictions of the format. The High Definition movie with surround sound will give you a completely different experience that the black and white. Essentials, like you, have the High Definition capability and your choice is whether you turn this capability on or not. In my experience, denying or avoiding your Essential capability yields discontent, frustration and eventually medical problems. More on this later.

Both ways of experiencing the world are great and serve vital roles. This is not about being better than another. Everyone is born with inherent value; it is what we do or don't do with that value that tells the story. The Essential's path offers challenges that the other path does not experience. Sometimes being an Essential is difficult and you might feel disconnected from others or even judged. Still your path is uniquely yours and part of your mission is to live from a place of compassion and gratitude for all life, including yours. Let's embrace all paths. If you are an Essential or visionary, I am confident you will find yourself in these pages.

In this book you will find questions to ponder and places to write your notes. Be willing to go within and tune into your deeper self as this is necessary for your health and happiness. Sometimes you may feel as if you are in an archeological dig, unearthing inner structures that are outdated and must be transformed. You will find information designed to answer common questions that I have been asked about being an Essential and I will offer time-tested solutions to assist you during your quest. I have included some stories in certain areas to demonstrate the message. They are based on real people yet are not the actual real people by name or identifiers. When you resonate with one of the people mentioned, rest assured that you are not alone. After all, this book is being written at the request of someone close to me who is an Essential who is making some noise! By noise, I mean using your Essential gifts for the advancement of a compassionate, unified way of living.

This book is meant to introduce new language and concepts. Many times, over the years I found myself looking for language to describe or communicate my experience and understanding and there were no words that were accurate. Taking the word Essential and using it as a noun has offered a new way to express these powerful and unique roles and gifts. An Essential is awakening and growing on levels known and unknown. Essentials have many questions and experiences. Having a safe place to turn and people who understand is vital. In this world of turbulence as the up-leveling of conscious is happening, Essentials are playing a vital role while also requiring additional support, recharging of inner energies of transformation, and a sense of being understood and connection. There is much more information than can be contained in this book. I am here to point out what has been happening around you your entire life and give it words and context. We all get to point out for each other what is already unfolding. We are like jumper cables for each other. This is part of the great awakening of which we are vital to the process. Start with Hope. Know that it is precisely in the deep dark that your new grace is born. From here, you experience a deep sense of knowing that words cannot describe.

You came here to create something powerful. You have the right to be here; to live and create from your inner vision.

Continue to learn, grow, and ask questions.

Chapter 1
What Does It Mean to Fit in Anyway?

> *Why fit in when you were born to stand out!*
> *~~Dr. Seuss*

The whole idea of fitting in has always been curious to me. Sometimes it seems that fitting in is desirable and other times not so much. What are the cultural rules? Do they apply to me? What if I have never really fit in even when others think I am?

I have come to realize that everyone fits in in their own unique and personal way. Fitting in with popular culture may not be your thing yet on the core-essence level, you fit in to the greater scheme of things.

For those of us who have a deep inner conviction or calling, and we are compelled from within to bring our vision forward; we are Essentials. Being an Essential can offer challenges that make life interesting. Chances are that the times you did not fit in or you thought no one understood you were the times your Essential gifts were shining brightly. Just because the masses may not understand you means nothing more than the masses don't understand. This is a statement about them, not you. You are fully equipped in your personal unique way to bring your Essential gifts into reality. You always have the free will choice to succumb to the energy a flow of the masses or to stand out and fit in in different ways.

Let's explore what an Essential is and some of the variations. Notice where you see yourself.

What is an Essential?

An Essential is a participant in the greater picture of Universal harmony. In general, Essentials are grounded in service and inspiration while also bringing in new ideas and creations that are ushering humankind forward. You may or may not understand the significance of your personal Essential gifts. Whether you are aware of not, your Essential gifts are within you and they are meant to emerge into the world and make noise in their personal and unique manner.

All Essentials have unique gifts that they must use to be an intentional presence in Universal harmony. Knowing that the Universe is always expanding in unity, diversity and complexity, Essentials are key players in this expanded consciousness. There are 5 types of variations of gifts; Essentials can have any combination and intensity of these variations.

The 5 variations include: Creators, Workers, Weavers, Harmonizers and Ballers. Each variation offers much needed energy and creative energy to our transforming world.

How to identify an Essential

Essentials are often service or mentor leaders regardless of position or age. Essentials share a common vision of a better world that has more peace, harmony, and light. The road toward this vision varies with each person's talents and calling, yet the overarching goal is the same: elevating personal and thus global consciousness in a sustainable manner.

Some Essentials are in the forefront of social justice, health care, environmental issues and humanitarian efforts to name a few. Some Essentials has deep rooted passions in these areas and their calling is to serve others from behind the scenes. Whatever your Essential variation, you are a perfect, unique combination of Essential gifts here with the vision, motivation and energy to make a difference.

There is no need to compare one Essential to another as they are interwoven and each variation of gifts support and is synchronous with the others. This is the magnificent beauty that erupts when Essentials come together in their vision and actions. The noise that a group of Essential makes is much like an orchestra who has been playing together for years. The harmony, blending of instruments and the music itself are inspiring can move mountains or often even the hardest hearts.

Do not underestimate the palpable personal power emanating through you that is meant to be of service. The wonder thing, for me, is that we all will bring our gifts forward with our personal flair. The brilliant diversity transcends what any one human can dream! Let's look at the variations. *Where do you fit in?*

The 5 Variations of Essentials

There are variations of Essentials. Each variation stands alone and simultaneously intermingles with the other variations. Each variation has a vital role and mission. Fitting in is an important task. How to fit in and where to fit in are valid considerations. In a world where taking the risk to stand up and express your powerful and authentic self can have daunting consequences, you must make noise in a way that serves the good of all, including yourself. If you feel you cannot be quiet anymore, or you have a burning push coming from deep within, you are an Essential.

Essentials come in every style imaginable. You always have the chance to bring your unique personality to your vision and mission. This is what is so exciting. When you are in a room of Essentials with similar gifts, you will be awed by the beauty of the varied expressions.

You could be a single variation of Essential or you may be a blending of multiple variations of Essential. Let's look at the 5 variations. Notice which ones resonate with you most profoundly. You may see yourself in more than one area.

Creators are connected to purpose and intention. Creators seek to know and understand the meaning of the manifest as well as the invisible world. They are often talking about purpose and having purpose. Creators use their power of intention as a navigating power for how they live their lives. Creators are asking the deeper questions and they become animated and more engaged when they connect with those who also care about these resonate on these deeper more philosophical levels.

Creators are often found in the metaphysical, theological or life's purpose professions. Creators become animated when talking about these more introspective yet purposeful topics. Creators often dislike small talk and they prefer intellectual conversations. May Creators are well read and have vast interest in the meaning of life and how to create a satisfying and successful life from having a sense of purpose and living that purpose.

Workers are the stabilizers who identify goals and consistently move forward. Workers are great strategists and planners. You will find workers excelling when they can plan the strategy to get the job done and then do the job. Workers are always moving and working for them is not work at all. Workers enjoy reaching goals then strategizing the next goal. Workers are the grounding and stabilizing force in the world of Essentials. They often interact more easily with others because of their focus on organization, and getting things done. Their inner life is powerful, and they have the compelling desire to do good work. Don't be fooled by their worker exterior, this group possess and inner passionate vision and life. They can get things done! Workers are fueled largely by their inner passion and ability to see the goal and get moving to achieve the goal.

Workers are found wherever there is a great vision that is being brought into reality. Often, workers will align with other essentials and bring their strategy and work ethic to the project. When a project needs to get done, call on the workers. Some workers I know struggle at times with their Essential gift. I have heard the perception that being the worker is somehow less than the others. Quite the contrary. Workers are necessary for any viable project to come together.

Workers have a drive to do the job and get it done well. Workers thrive when there is something to accomplish that is tangible and can be measured. Workers are the perfect complement for the other Essentials as they can bring solutions and practical ideas and action that may elude others at some points.

Weavers bridge ideas and concepts by being in the flow of creativity and spiritual essence. They bring ideas into existence. Weavers can be found often in a teaching type capacity whether formal or informal. Weavers have the ability to naturally distill complex concepts into manageable parts, while also taking pieces of concepts and synthesizing them. Weavers are vital to any enterprise or group because of their communication skills. They are the translators who understand various worldviews and orientations in order to achieve a universal understanding. Think of a beautiful tapestry: The threads and yarns are beautiful alone, but it is the Weaver who makes the collective beauty come alive.

Weavers have the natural ability to bring ideas and concepts together from the esoteric to the grounded in natural reality. When you listen to a public speaker who seems to resonate with the entire audience, you are listening to a weaver. Weavers can be found in ministry, public speaking, teaching, law and the sciences. The Weaver Essential gift is a variation that often amazes others. They are often hear comments like, "How did you take that enormous concept and make it manageable to understand?" Weavers tend to want to learn many varied viewpoints and they can easily move from view to view when engaged in a team. Weavers can bridge the visionaries with the workers and the strategists with the creators. Weavers can create a sense of beauty and wonder where it once was hidden by bringing together the raw essence.

Weavers are often graceful and can be seen as elegant and flowing in their demeanor. Much like the pliable yarn in the tapestry, Weavers naturally are comfortable examining and engaging in varied activities and dialogues. The Weavers' translation and interpretation ability comes naturally. Weavers can offer perspective to a situation or project.

Harmonizers are playful and lighthearted, living in the flow, smoothing out the rough edges of life. They are like instruments in an orchestra emanating the feeling of beauty and harmony that often transcends words. You can hear their inner calm in their voice, and you can sense their light when around them. Somehow, we feel more peaceful and connected when they are around. Harmonizers are in the flow of eternal fluidity. This means that Harmonizers inherently move in the eternal flow of life with grace and ease. Harmonizers bring out the inner joy and sense of play in those around them. Harmonizers are like beautiful music that embraces your mind, body, and soul with its intricate melody. Harmonizers have the natural ability to dissipate tension and bring about consensus as they can connect deeply to the underlying intentions and bring about great transformation using lighthearted measures. This ability is most valuable in teamwork and situations where others express passionate ideas that, left alone, could derail a wonderful project.

Harmonizers are the lighthearted and spirited people who can break any tension with ease. They use humor and their playful mannerisms to add levity to the seriousness of the other Essentials, particularly the Ballers. Harmonizers gravitate toward meditation, yoga, Tai Chi and other harmonizing activities. Harmonizers are sensitive to strife and discord that they typically avoid or shift using their Essential gifts. Sometimes Harmonizers can get so lost in the flow that the Workers or Ballers are helpful in creating a plan and taking action. Harmonizers are great with the melody of life and they always bring this powerful perspective. They balance the energy of any situation easily.

Ballers are dialed into relentless sources of energy. They often possess raw, unadulterated power. Ballers are the risk-takers and creators of unlimited power. Many visionaries are sub-categories of Ballers. They are uncommon and know things beyond others. Often this group is misunderstood by most of those around them. When a Baller is connected to the unlimited power source of the Universe, it can be overwhelming for them as well as those around them.

Ballers are by nature go-getters and action-takers. They have tremendous energy and drive. Ballers can't stop this energy or drive without dire health consequences like hypertension, digestion problems and sleep issues. Without Ballers and their extreme action orientation, any progress and transformation would at a slower pace.

Ballers are often misunderstood by those who only look at the outside persona. Often, their hearts are soft, and they love so deeply that taking action seems like the only way to fulfill this burning inner furnace. Ballers often have difficulty connecting with others or healing grief. Ballers are moving so fast that slowing down can be painful for them. This rapid inner speed shields them from some of the emotional intensity and healing that may need to happen for their health. Ballers are all about taking massive action no matter what. It usually takes someone with several variations/gifts to actually understand and connect to a Baller. Yet, Ballers are the powerhouse and they bring great amounts of information, higher understanding and energy to any project or relationship.

You will find Ballers is high level business that requires, vision, action and a relentless amount of personal energy to champion the mission. Some Ballers burn out and end up struggling with anger, frustration, intolerance and self-centeredness. A healthy Baller who engages in appropriate self-care is a force that cannot be easily stopped. Ballers dislike long meetings and people who talk to hear themselves talking. Ballers get to the point, focus on action and results. They are valuable to any team. They also have a strong sense of service and the vision to bring about much needed transformation or change.

What to consider

What is most important is for Essentials to delve within to be clear on their personal variation and then bring their essential nature into the light in a powerful manner. By bringing out your essential nature as an Essential, you make the powerful noise that changes things for the better. Always, you are living in your Essential gift when your vision, words and actions are for the highest good of all concerned. Most likely, you found yourself in more than one or maybe all 5 Essentials.

Notice where you resonated or were disconnected. The variations and expressions of each Essential variations are endless in diversity and complexity. These brief descriptions are designed to offer an overview of the general categories of Essentials.

In the following chapters, I will delve further into each variation of Essential in more detail.

Questions to Ponder:

With which Essential variation do you most identify?

Which Essential variation do you see in others in your life?

How does it benefit you to identify and step into your Essential variation?

Journal your ideas and inspirations:

Chapter 2
The Creators

Creators are connected to purpose and intention. Creators seek to know and understand the meaning of the manifest as well as the invisible world. They are often talking about purpose and having purpose.

Creators use their power of intention as their navigating force. Creators are asking the deeper questions and they become animated and more engaged when they connect with those who also care about these matters.

Creators live with purpose on purpose. Creators speak about the higher, often existential matters of existence. Creators long for someone to connect with on these deeper matters. Creators are the Essential variation who use intention to expand awareness and thus expand the consciousness of humanity.

Creators bring out their inner vision and are clear on their vision and calling. Conversation styles are centered around purpose in a spiritual sense rather than only a physical sense.

Creators manifest things. Creators see the creation needed and then use the power of intention to bring it into reality. Creators remind us of the power in our words and how to live with intention. Work and action are not foreign to Creators as they are known to take focused action based on their inner insights.

Creators can be found in spiritual studies like Dr. Wayne Dyer and Louise Hay as well as in business. Dave Sandoval, founder of Purium, is a Creator. Arts and Entertainment have Creators as well. Gwen Steffani and Madonna are two examples that come to mind and there are many more. They use their Creator variation as the launching place for their music careers. Many others bring the power of thought and intention while using the Creator variation to support their primary variation.

Creators are helpful with seeing the vision and sharing that vision as part of an overall project or plan. They will be focused on doing the right thing and maintaining integrity. If you are a Creator, use your variation wisely. You are creating your life based on your thoughts. Be sure they are high vibration thoughts rather than low vibration of fear, anger, sadness or guilt. If you know a Creator, support their vision by listening deeply and offer support or encouragement. Whatever your relationship with the Creator Essential variation, enjoy what is created.

Meet Samuel

Samuel is a 34-year-old student of life. Studying formally and informally for the majority of his lifetime. He recounts learning to meditate and create with experience in the third grade. He began to work with me to assist him in focusing more succinctly on his vision and creating his heart's desire for his life. Samuel shared with me his rocky toad and times of not being understood by his peers.

Samuel reported suffering from depression and feeling loneliness within his peer group. His conversation was largely existential and focused on higher ideals and delving deep within his being to connect more fully. He had studied many religions and philosophical views and is focused on incorporating increased harmony and joy into his life using the teachings he is practicing.

Samuel can be found studying matters of existence and intention. Samuel uses his awareness of the power of intention to illuminate his experience. Samuel shared with me that he has been ridiculed for considering intention and purpose when setting his goals. He states he has learned over time to follow what resonates with himself and continue to focus on his purpose.

Most of Samuel's peers are actually his senior as he does not readily relate to his chronological peers, Samuel uses cartoons and fantasy to stimulate his thinking. He is an avid documentary viewer where he relates what he is learning to his personal vision. Samuel becomes excited and animated when I ask about the latest documentary and how the information relates to him.

Samuel's variation of Creator assists him in creating opportunities that expand his consciousness. Samuel is known by his colleagues and friends as someone who can focus and create his desired outcomes. He uses his inner Creator variation to bring to fruition his goals and desires.

Samuel needs to also be aware that his variation of Creator applies in all directions. Wherever his focus goes, energy flows and new things are created. Samuel has learned over time to be discerning about where his energy flows. Because the Universe freely gives according to our thoughts, words and intentions, Samuel focuses regularly in our meetings on his thinking patterns and how they align to his inner vision and what he is creating with his thoughts.

For Samuel, being a Creator Essential can be challenging and exhilarating. He is learning more about his other variations that support his Creator variation and he is working on allowing all of him to show up in the world. Working through the grief of being bullied and misunderstood years ago can show up as an echo of days gone by. Samuel is focused and resilient as he continues to excavate what is not serving him and replace his creative ability with compassion, kindness and self-love.

As this book is bring published, Samuel is focused on the intersection of being a Creator and his love of engineering and computer science. He is curious and our conversations yield great insights as he moves forward. Samuel recently shared that he is grateful to have someone who understands him in his corner!

Questions to Ponder:

How do you identify with Samuel?

Whom do you know that could be the variation Creator?

What aspects, if any, of Creator do you see in yourself?

Journal your ideas and inspirations:

Chapter 3
The Workers

Workers are the stabilizers who identify goals and consistently move forward. Workers are great strategists and planners. You will find workers excelling when they develop strategies to get the job done and then do the job. Workers are always moving and working for them is not work at all. Workers enjoy strategizing, organizing, and reaching goals. They make the best generals, marketers, and businesspeople.

Workers have the grounding forces in the world of Essentials. They can often interact more easily with others because the focus for them is more tangible results. Their inner life is powerful and the compelling desire to do good work is palpable. Don't be fooled by the what is merely on the outside within this group, they are passionate and can get things done!

Workers are the stabilizing ones. They are grounded and able to set clear realistic goals and work for them. The workers enjoy working and may not even call their work, work. Workers are great goal setters. They do not miss much, and their focus is comprehensive.

Workers are a valuable Essential because of their work ethic and unrelenting focus on community and global projects. Need something done? Call a Worker Essential and you can be assured that the goals will be clear and that the tasks will get done.

All groups need Worker Essentials. When you are in the flow of the Worker Essential, you are joy filled with the work you are doing and results seem to flow easily in many ways, even if the actual work is difficult.

Meet Richard

Richard sought my advice due to feeling stressed and burned out to the point where he was having heart problems. Richard did not care for himself spiritually, physically or emotionally in his younger days and he suffered from a heart attack at age 30. Lifestyle and stress appeared to be the culprit. Currently, a 55-year-old successful entrepreneur, he was struggling with literally working himself to death. He reluctantly asked for help following his wife and adult children urging him to take action for his health.

Richard has been an industrious and hard-working person since his youth. Always planning and working. He had not yet learned balance and ways to take care of himself as he developed in his Essential role. We worked on healing old toxic beliefs about work and being responsible. As we began to unravel his inner dialogue that was adding stress to his life, Richard reported feeling more powerful in his work because he could focus and was sleeping progressively better as he practiced new skills that supported his Worker Essential variation rather than drive him deeper into desperation.

In his early years, Richard struggled with resentment over working more than others around him. He could not yet see the stability and grounding of his variation. All he could see was that others did not seem to work as much as he was working. As we explored the other variations and Richard could also see some of the variations in himself, he began to release old resentments and blame that had been plaguing his daily thoughts.

Richard made some inner changes with his thinking and in his lifestyle and he started feeling better. His mood was more elevated and his words optimistic as he could feel relief from the pressure being built up inside.

Today, Richard is thriving in his Worker Essential variation, working and enjoying the products of his work. He is the grounding force in his family and business. By honoring his variation of being a Worker, Richard has found solace that he is living his soul's mission. In this knowing, he has added much richness and peace to his inner world.

Richard also offers grounding support and advice to his children and he is enjoying greater connection with others the moment he had the awakening to his variation and how he can use it to his benefit. He noted that with clarity and understanding comes peace and calm.

Work makes Richard happy and he loves to strategize and complete projects. His business is flourishing, and he is working on new projects that feed his soul. Richard can now accept support and guidance from other Essentials, and he is adept at discerning valuable opportunities now that his system has more equilibrium.

Questions to Ponder:

Do you identify with Richard?

Whom do you know that could be the variation Worker?

What aspects, if any, of Worker do you see in yourself?

Journal your ideas and inspirations:

Chapter 4
The Weavers

Weavers bridge ideas and concepts by being in the creative flow and weaving the flow with form to bring forth manageable concepts and ideas. They bring ideas into daily reality as if they are grabbing the content from a Higher source and distilling it into a beautiful tapestry. Weavers can be found often in a teaching-type capacity whether formal or informal. They are the translators and can understand divergent world views and orientations. They focus on the achievement of Universal understanding. I always think of a beautiful tapestry when I am around a Weaver. The threads and yarns are beautiful alone but is the Weaver that makes the collective beauty come alive.

Being around a weaver is a magical experience. Weavers bring together diverse concepts by bridging viewpoints, energies and perspectives. For me, Weaver Essential energy is awe inspiring and elegant. I just love watching the picture come together as they assemble to pieces in perfect order with an ease and grace.

Weavers are great on a team because they assimilate the ideas and energies of the group's intention and weave together the group's vision with the available resources. Weavers are usually flowing as they move from task to task. Their walk is kind and gentle and they move with an obvious rhythm.

Weavers can take many pieces and bring them together into a synergistic and powerful whole. An Essential-Weaver can create a thing of beauty right before your eyes. I think of monks creating a sand mandala as a beautiful Weaver manifestation. Often the power of the creation transcends words.

Weavers can bridge the larger pictures and digest the critical concepts for consumption by others. They also take the larger concepts and create miniatures that are manageable for themselves and others. By taking the pieces and creating a work of beauty, the Weaver brings a powerful and strong presence in our world.

Weavers bring ideas into daily reality. Weavers are amazing manifestors, often working closely with Creators for beneficial results. Chances are many of the ideas you see manifest in day to day life were woven together and then brought forward by a Weaver. Their ability is a thing of beauty to watch and experience.

CHAPTER 4

Meet Betty

Betty is an Essential Weaver variation. She is bright and curious, always looking thigs up to learn more. She often is aware of up and coming information and breakthroughs in science and other areas of knowledge. Betty has developed a broad knowledge base through reading, video and other activities. Betty is always drawing her ideas or writing when she is not sharing with others. Betty is a powerful Weaver in that she bridges divergent viewpoints and finds common ground while weaving together the value.

Betty is known to me through sailing circles. We sail together at times and I am always in awe of her breadth of knowledge about the sport and collateral information like tide and weather. Betty is a deep listener and she is able to hear what is not being said and then take appropriate action during the sailboat race. Betty also uses her Weaver Essential gift in her personal world.

Betty relates to the teenagers in the neighborhood and the yacht club who are seeking to be heard and understood, teaching them the value of tradition while also teaching them how to expand and be who they are meant to be. Betty weaves together health information and uses cutting-edge ideas to support her family and friends. Often, she will make changes because of research and taking a deep dive into a particular topic, such as healthy eating. I remember Betty talking about healthy versus unhealthy fats before the conversation ever hit the media. Betty shared that she had been studying the topic for a few months after reading a short article. Her deep dive and her Weaver ability to take the information and make it readily accessible to others is certainly the Weaver gift in action. She then shares understandable actions that are a direct result of the information, weaving together the concepts and healthy action.

Betty's presence is strong yet non-abrasive. She is confident and allays others' fears by deeply listening and using her Weaver Essential variation to support and care for others. I imagine this is why teenagers and those who feel misunderstood come to Betty for counsel. I have watched her listen for long periods of time to friends and teammates. She always seems to have a great synthesis to share to help direct the person or situation.

Weavers like Betty are vital to the expansion of human consciousness. Weavers offer the necessary glue and substance that ties things together so that the overall puzzle comes together in a meaningful manner. Without the Weaver Essential variation, the bringing together of vision and action would be quite fascinating. Weavers, like Betty, help us save time and challenges by offering the picture of the situation in meaningful ways along with actionable steps to take.

Betty shared with me recently that she has had sometimes of disillusionment over her lifetime until she was able to embrace her gift and use it to serve others. She told me that caring for others and being a guide has helped her improve her self-care and her focus on what she offers instead of what she thinks is lacking.

I believe that this type of process is common among Essentials. Going from unknown to known to living on purpose takes work, faith, trust and daily actions. I am grateful to know Betty and see the positive impact she so naturally offers.

Questions to Ponder:

Do you identify with Betty?

Whom do you know that could be the variation Weaver?

What aspects, if any, of Weaver do you see in yourself?

Journal your ideas and inspirations:

Chapter 5
The Harmonizers

Harmonizers are playful and lighthearted, living in the flow, smoothing out the rough edges of life. They are like the instruments in an orchestra vibrating with beauty. You can hear their inner calm in their voice, and you can feel it when you are around them. Somehow, you feel more peaceful and connected when they are around.

Harmonizers are in the flow of eternal fluidity. Harmonizers bring out the inner joy and play in those around them. Harmonizers are like beautiful music that embraces your mind, body and soul with an equalizing and beautiful melody. Their beautiful harmonizing melody enters your life in the difficult spaces and offers you an internal healing and restorative salve for your body and soul.

Harmonizers have the natural ability to dissipate tension and bring about consensus as they can connect deeply to the underlying intentions and bring about great transformation using their lighthearted presence and demeanor. This ability is most valuable is teams and situations where there are others who are intense mentally and emotionally and that intensity, if left alone could overpower or even derail a great vision.

If you want to learn how to be excellent at living in the moment, observe and learn from a Harmonizer. Their grounding and soothing vibe is a transformative combination that is ultimately nourishing to your soul. Every Baller and Worker Essential variation works well with Harmonizers who smooth out the rough edges of life.

You can hear inner calm in their voice, and you can sense it when you are around them. Somehow, you feel more peaceful and connected when an Essential Harmonizer is around. They are like the instruments in an orchestra bringing together beautiful melodies that are an auditory and often visceral experience.

Harmonizers must develop healthy, firm boundaries. Their harmonizing impact does not consist of smoothing over in an act of denial or avoidance. Rather, a Harmonizer's energy brings together and flows through situations and groups, harmonizing as it moves onward. Think of a beautiful song that touches your heart and soul, this was most likely created by a Harmonizer!

Harmonizers tend to live in a comfortable flow. Their playful nature supports and tempers the often-high intensity of other variations of Essentials. Harmonizers are vitally important as they can meld into varied undulations and tempos to bring a harmony and a peace to any group or project. Often, they are soul-filled musicians or poets. I think of Emily Dickinson, Carol King, Ellen DeGenerous, Elizabeth Barret Browning, James Taylor and Michael Bublé to name a few. Their words and melodies touch you deep within where words may escape you. As you experience them and their Harmonizer gifts, your inner landscape enjoys a beautiful bath of harmony.

Meet David

David is a sailing friend who has an amazing calming influence on racing sailboats which can be an intense environment. He brings a sense of playfulness in his smile and his quirky comments. He supports the team and he is competent in performing his position of the competitive team. Harmonizers can be very focused and competitive while brings a flow and levity when needed for the greater success of the team. His demeanor has uniquely positioned him to be able to use his Essential Harmonizer variation in a way that includes and brings people together.

David and I have spent many social hours together. He brings his Harmonizer gift to social events where he can sooth my stressful day with his smile and gentle comments. David has clear, respectful boundaries which allows his friends and family to trust his comforting presence. He has many friends from many walks of life, and they all comment on how they feel around him. His Harmonizer gift is prevalent, even though I am not sure he sees the value and power in his Essential Harmonizer gift.

David is the quick to offer assistance, whether it is help moving, sharing information or offering a listening ear. He has been there for me with my intensities often over the years. Harmonizers live up to their name and they typically leave an interaction elevated.

When David speaks, the flow of grace and calm ushers from his lips in both his words and tone. His smile is infectious. David is a professional in the investment business who allows his essential variation to be present in his daily interactions. He is an entrepreneur and he flows through work demands with poise and a quiet confidence. Many people have strong emotions about money due to their beliefs. The old baggage they carry can become challenging for any advisor. David uses his Essential Harmonizer gift to help ease clients' minds and they are then able to understand their choices and options with clarity.

This harmonizing flow can also be seen in his family. He smiles and has a calm assurance about his words and actions. David is on point and maintains connections and is actively present in their lives. He is present and attentive with his friends and community as well. David brings together generations with a harmonizing impact on relationships.

David's Essential Harmonizer variation uniquely poises him to bring the fun and heart felt dimension into the world. Harmonizers, like David, are valuable assets to the Essentials for without their influence, equilibrium and hope could seem elusive.

Questions to Ponder:

Do you identify with David?

Whom do you know that could be the variation Harmonizer?

What aspects, if any, of Harmonizer do you see in yourself?

Journal your ideas and inspirations:

Chapter 6
The Ballers

Ballers are dialed into a relentless source of energy. They are often raw, unadulterated power. Ballers are the risk takers and creators of unlimited power. They are uncommon and tend to know things beyond what others may imagine. Often this group is misunderstood or not understood by most of those around them. When a Baller is connected to the unlimited power source of the Universe it can be overwhelming for them as well as others at times.

Sometimes they may say that there are so many ideas and things to do and experience that they freeze. This seeming paralysis and inability to process and move forward can cause inner turmoil. Some Ballers I work with struggle with the overload of information and ideas that can be overwhelming. Once they begin to master the Essential Baller gift, all the rules change, and they excel magnificently.

Ballers are by nature go getters and action takers. They have tremendous energy and drive. Ballers can't stop this energy or drive without dire health consequences. Without Ballers things would evolve much slower. Ballers are often misunderstood by those who only look at the outside persona. Often, their hearts are soft, and they love so deeply that taking action seems like the only way to relieve this burning inner furnace. It releases the inner energy and offers relief.

Ballers often have difficulty with connecting with others or healing grief. It usually takes someone with several variations of Essential gifts to actually understand and connect to a Baller. Yet, Ballers are the powerhouses and they bring great amounts of information, higher understanding and energy to any project or relationship.

Caring too deeply and not taking good care of self or being unhealthy and dysfunctional in other ways can yield to high-level dysfunction and problems. Ballers are susceptible to personality disorders as well as addiction in many forms. Power, greed, control, fear, pity are addictions that Ballers can experience along with alcohol and other substances.

Intuitive visionaries could be considered a sub-category of this, the powerhouse variation of Essentials. They speak the truth from dimensions that many others may not understand. They are uncommon and know things beyond obvious realms. Others may make comments like, "She just knows things." Often this group is misunderstood or not understood in many everyday settings.

Boundaries and learning when and how to speak can be a real challenge for this group. Because they can see things others cannot. Their road can sometimes be tricky. Once the others experience the power and accuracy of the Intuitive Baller, they appear to be willing to work and come together. Examples here include Ron Howard, Albert Einstein, Barbara Walters, Walt Disney and Richard Branson. These people are a mighty force that can be used in many forms.

Meet Alexandra (Alex)

Alex has been marching to the beat of a different drummer since she was a child. She went "all out" in her activities and had remarkable energy. Alex took risks from the time she can remember. She was often getting into trouble with her strict parents because of her endless mischievousness.

Alex had interests in the arts, sports and many different things. She was able to do her chores and still had the focus and drive to engage in what interested her. Alex was a Baller, driven and full of energy.

I met Alex at an event when we were in college. She was a go-getter, and everyone knew this about her. I was always moving and busy, but Alex seemed to be operating on another level. She was focused on achievement. She had a double major and excelled in her athletic pursuits while making straight A's. We became fast friends because of our connection around taking action and getting things accomplished.

We were varied in that I had more intuitive and Weaver Essential variation while Alex was more about resources and getting things accomplished. We enjoy our Essential variations today in our ongoing friendship.

Alex was different from most Ballers in that she was not the typical larger than life personality, yet she was larger than life in her drive, focus and motivation to get things accomplished. She was a formidable presence as an athlete and musician in addition to her exceptional professional career as the Chief Operating Officer for a large corporation. Her raw energy and drive could be seen in her business prowess as well as her talents in sports and music. She excels at everything she attempts and remains on top of her game.

Alex enjoys sharing the results of her success in various philanthropic endeavors. As a Baller variation, Alex follows her inner calling and heart's desire to be of service and use her wealth and prominence in the community to be a leader in the areas of social welfare and sustainability for the generations to come.

Questions to Ponder:

Do you identify with Alex?

Whom do you know that could be the variation Baller?

What aspects, if any, of Baller do you see in yourself?

Journal your ideas and inspirations:

Chapter 7
The Development of an Essential

We ought to live sacrificing, and singing, and dancing.
~~Plato

All Essentials grow and develop from infancy through adulthood in atypical ways when related to the norm. As you look back on your life, you will notice times and areas when you were progressing at a different pace than those around you. You may also have noticed that you experience intensities in intellect, emotions, physicality that seems to set you apart.

I once worked with an Essential who was in his forties. He said he felt like his life was finally coming together. After 3 different careers and endeavors, he said he is now braiding together them together into a fulfilling vocation with meaning and purpose. He now sees that what he thought was wasted time was not wasted time at all.

Developmental differences can create a wide variety in engagement and responses to the environment. Essentials often can be included in the conversation about being gifted. Being gifted is not simply about high IQ. Being gifted encompasses a wide array of challenges, abilities and deviations from typical, normal development.

For example, several gifted Essentials that I have worked with over the years started talking later than the average. Some started walking unusually early while still others have strong sensitivities to noise, movement or fabric of clothing. One common place is that no two Essentials are the same and everyone who is an Essential has personal signature of qualities, abilities and challenges.

Essentials have times of frustration with themselves and others. This can stem from processing delays or executive functioning challenges or intensities in life experience. Great athletes who may have a physical intensity that complements their Worker or Creator Essential variation. The combination can be endless.

Many Essentials have cyclical productivity. Some will say they are on or off and rarely in between. Some Essentials struggle with being vulnerable and may have mood swings or a mood heaviness that seems to follow them from a young age. Still other Essentials have a hunger and thirst from high ideas and spiritual awakening conversations and experiences.

I am sure you are getting my point. The development of each Essential is a varied, complex and unique as each person themselves. There are no cookie cutters and no single paradigm that fit all Essentials. You, as an Essential, are vital to the health and wellbeing of the world we find ourselves in today. No, you are not here to save the world. That idea is much too ego driven to be from an Essential. The savior idea which many recoils from and others seek is simply an egoic construct. Even great spiritual leaders have not said they were here to save the world. They say they are here in Love, bringing a message that the kingdom of God is within, that Happiness is a religion, that the Golden Rule in all languages remains the same and that respecting Earth and all sentient beings is vital from survival. Following the example and ideals of the greats invites us to step up and live life from a deeper place of inner integrity. Essentials are the group who can, with confidence, bring a more enlightened way of living to everyday life. Let's examine what this looks like.

Meet Blanche

Blanche always had a sense that she was different. When she was a little girl, the adults called her "different" and "special". Her friends seemed to be confused at times event though she would get along with them just fine. As Blanche reflected on the morning, afternoon and now evening of her life, she recounted fond memories dotted with some real painful challenges. Blanche granted the interview with me under the condition that I keep her name anonymous. So, I asked a friend for a random name, so Blanche it is. There is a piece of Blanche in each of us. See where you identify your paths.

Blanche has several college degrees, Chemistry, Anthropology, Theology and Philosophy. She also has studied other sciences and history. Blanche shared that she loves to learn, both formally and informally. She smiled as she shared about her high school sweetheart. She still longs for him. He left for the war and he never came home. She cried as she told the story of their last good-bye as teenagers in love. She remembers not wanting him to leave but he said he had to serve his country. I could feel her deep pain as she shared this story with me decades later.

Blanche pursued her vocation in industrial psychology and the psychology of marketing in a large firm in New York City. Moving was a hard thing, she said, but she had to get out of her hometown to help heal the pain of her loss. Blanche fondly remembered her first co-workers and

CHAPTER 7

her adjustment to city life. Sometimes, she would stay up all night having fun with her new friends. Sometimes, she would be more a recluse, going within for find her meaning.

Blanche was a Harmonizer Essential. She showed me many of her cherished possessions from her youth, including the engraving plate from her graduation. She was the first woman in her family to receive a college degree. She was so proud. Blanche loved to learn and had several books on her coffee table as we spoke. All of which she reports currently reading.

The purpose of our meeting was for an interview about Essentials and to listen to her journey and connections. I asked her about this idea and how she resonated with the ideas. Blanche, freely shared her experiences which included gymnastics competitions, spelling bees, writing several fiction books and a non-fiction book, getting married and having 3 children. She has a couple of grandchildren too! Blanche told me she was happy to allow me to interview her as she wanted to share some ideas about the evening of life. Blanche and I spoke for hours, relating stories and laughing and crying. What a glorious day.

Blanche lights up when speaking about her family. She also shared some pain that would cover her mood from time to time in longing for her first love. She said her husband and children all know her story. Blanche has a level of openness and mischievousness that comes through her smile and her brilliant blue eyes.

Blanche spent years as a stay at home mom while creating ideas and art in her quiet moments. She also taught school and enjoyed the students. Blanche was the mom in the neighborhood that every teenager came to for a listening ear. She showed me some old photos. She was ginning ear to ear. Blanche became a high-powered CEO for a large corporation when her children were all school aged and beyond. She loved her family life and she loved her vocational life because they filled different needs for her.

Blanche is a wise, talented and accomplished woman. She has some of each Essential I her and she learned over the years to let he authentic light shine. Blanche played a song on her piano as she reminisced on her life. She lovingly said, "I wouldn't change a thing." A Baller in her corporate life while balancing with being a Creator and Weaver in her creative life while using her Worker and Harmonizer in her family life, Blanche is a great example of how the Essential gifts come together in each Essential is different ways. I trust Blanche will inspire you to dig deep within to honor and express your inherent Essential Variations. Blanche's legacy continues through her children and the people whom she has touched with her loving and kind presence.

Essentials develop differently. Everyone has the perfect combination of gifts. Essentials are here to make the world a more enlightened, loving and peaceful place from the inside out. Whether you are aware of it or not, you are fully equipped and uniquely qualified to express your Essential self. Put yourself in position to receive your blessing.

Write some of your story. Note your Essential gifts and how they are showing up today. Share some of your story with a trusted other. How do you feel?

___

___

___

___

___

___

___

___

___

___

___

___

___

___

___

___

___

___

___

___

___

___

___

Chapter 8
Things to Consider for Each Essential Variation

For Essentials, there are challenges, obstacles or issues that can surface that do not serve the greater good and in fact could have negative consequences. Yes, being an Essential is an awesome gift and at the same time there are also some liabilities to consider. Every Essential, when out of balance or dysfunctional, can experience problems and can cause problems for others.

One of the goals of this book is to encourage you to embrace your Essential variation while also doing the work to be free of the bondage of old ideas, beliefs, paradigms and unresolved pain. When an Essential is unhealthy and out of balance, harm can happen, and this is not the role of Essentials. So, we must do the work. We must heal old wounds. We must offer forgiveness and compassion to ourselves and others. We must establish and maintain healthy mental, emotional, physical and spiritual boundaries within and without. It is our responsibility as an Essential to open our inner gift and make healthy noise!!

Unresolved grief and emotions such as fear, doubt, pain and worry can cause discord and disconnection from your authentic purpose. When these toxic emotions are coloring your reality and blocking your Higher connection, you can easily come out of alignment and create increased challenges for you and others. You will experience emotional dysregulation and you will struggle with maintaining a healthy life free from burn out.

A closed heart can keep people and situations away from you that can help further your calling as an Essential. Unresolved pain and separation cause blockages around your heart that then acts as a block to the good that wants to enter. In our world, you must freely open your heart and invite in your vision and to do this consistently working to take down those inner walls is vital to your success and happiness.

Grabbing or yearning to the point of becoming weary repels the very thing you are seeking. I had a friend who wanted to get married so bad that every time she met a man, she grabbed on to him and became controlling, suspicious and demanding. In short, order the new man would leave and she would be left looking once again. I helped he see that her grabbing type energy was like taking an emotional hostage rather than inviting in e new person. One she relaxed and healed her unresolved relationship grief, she stopped taking hostages. She is now in a happy relationship because there is balance and the old pain and grief is not driving her behavior and emotions.

Essentials, in all variations, must follow their inner compulsion to continue to grow and expand awareness and understanding. It is this expansion that allows for transformation and the ongoing progression of service and positive impact. Essentials are here on Earth to be a beneficial presence and help usher in a consciousness of unity and compassion. Essentials are called upon to become as healthy emotionally, physically, mentally and spiritually as possible because this job requires discernment, good boundaries and a solid foundation upon which to stand.

Essentials, for me, are the superheroes of today. They may be heralded in many ways and may come from any belief or corner of the Earth. What is true for each Essential is the deep inner conviction that is being birthed with every "Yes!"

There are important questions to ask yourself as you step more fully into your role as an Essential. Take time to answer these questions honestly following a time of inner reflection. Keep in mind, the more open and available you are, these responses change over time as you grow and transform. What was true for you earlier on your path may no longer be true today. Expansion is part of our experience. Allow your expansion and redirect limiting thinking toward expansion rather than restriction. You may have asked similar questions before.

Take time now and see what your inner self has to say. You may be surprised.

I find myself in the following Essential variations.

_____

_____

_____

_____

CHAPTER 8

How do I experience my Essential variation through sight?

_____
_____
_____
_____

How do I experience my Essential variation through smell?

_____
_____
_____
_____

How do I experience my Essential variation through physical sensations?

_____
_____
_____
_____

How do I experience my Essential variation through taste?

_____
_____
_____
_____

How do I experience my Essential variation through sound?

_____
_____
_____
_____

How do I experience my Essential variation through intuition or my heart?

_____

_____

_____

_____

The magnetizing and connecting power of the Universe is alive within you. Knowing this will help you live your authentic Truth. We are all connected and being called to awaken and move forward into a greater understanding and experience of life. All Essentials and variations are here on purpose to serve a grand role. Playing small or being quiet no longer serves to help uplift and evolve humanity. Repressing or trying to ignore your deeper nature creates anger, angst, depression and illness. Let's get going.

Take a minute and look at your own path and story. You know something new is happening when you realize that what once defined you, what was once your primary identity marker, is not coming with you into the next chapter of your life. Primary markers of identity are how you know who you are, such as your job, your family role, your interests, and your community for example. They are the ways you define yourself and your purpose. And now, you are poised to release the old identity markers as you embrace a new way of life, thus is the way of the Essential. Your path requires being aware of what parts of your identity will serve you moving forward and what parts of your identity will be released so the new may become manifest.

There are aspects of your persona and schema that remain and carry through from season to season. Remember when you needed a certain title or status? You are in the process of realizing that you no longer need that title or status to fulfill your vision. You are becoming free of the title or role you once played. This time of transcendence in your life is affording you the opportunity to be free of the old rules and bondage as you move into a more complete expression of you.

There are disruptions, things change, and you no longer need that title as the basis of your primary identity marker or value. You are going through a change. The question now becomes: "Will you open up and expand or will you narrow and restrict"? Many Essentials are known for inclusion of other paths and beliefs while releasing the restricting way of living that was once their primary identity. As an Essential, you are shedding the need for the outdated paradigms and boxes you once found comfortable. Your very presence here is a statement that you are a torchbearer in many ways. Surrendering to the flow of the Universe or is where your power as an Essential thrives and serves the greater Good.

It is time to release your burdens. What you fundamentally oriented yourself around in beliefs can now be released and the burden lifted. It is like taking off a tight shoe at the end of a long day! It is time to run all your decisions through your connection with Source. Pay attention to your inspired ideas and allow yourself to follow the promptings. Your natural humility emerges, and you become a new being as you allow the shedding of what no longer serves, and you expand into your next iteration. This process is always happening. You may only notice milestones, yet your expansion is *always* happening.

This newfound freedom is exhilarating and comes with additional responsibility. Stepping more fully into your mission means that you are accountable for your use of your Essential powers and gifts. Using your inherent gifts to bring about more enlightenment and expansion for humanity may be challenging. You are up to the challenge. You arrived on the planet fully equipped and able to fulfill your soul's mission and calling. This is where your inner "yes" enters.

You are, in some deep and mysterious way, partners with the universal energy that flows in and through all creation. You have co-creative power to positively impact your world and all beings. You are a gift to the world. It is time to think, speak, and act in alignment with the higher spiritual laws and are emerging from deep within your soul. When you do what seems to be good for you and the Divine, you are holding life with a lightness rather than closing off or shutting down. To be successful, be open, pay attention and never give up. If you are off, you will know it. Adjust your course accordingly and keep moving.

If you find yourself conflicted, meditate, pray and listen to your deeper self. Seek out wisdom, listen to your intuition and listen to what is deep within you. Always begin with the idea that your decisions and actions seem good to you and the Divine. Never claim that you "got this." Instead, be humble, open and willing to adjust as you move along your path. Do your work in discerning and act according to your inner guidance and connection with the Divine, Universal Source. With feedback from the Universe, you can always change your mind and approach things in a new way at any time.

You are on a journey and part of the journey includes leaving your comfort zone. It may mean moving away or changing peer groups. In any event, you begin a journey that you cannot resist. It keeps calling you. Then you notice how restless you are becoming with each passing day. You know there is a path you must walk and to deny this would be even more painful than the changes you need to make to take the journey. Your restlessness takes over until you follow your path.

Struggle and disillusionment that comes from the overwhelm and confusion of the new path and what to do and how to do what you are being led to do. Within this is the dark night of the soul. This is the time of powerful transformation as Spirit opens you up and breaks off what is not serving the highest good as you then begin your new path with renewed hope and focus. When you want to pull in and restrict and be protective, this is the time to be generous and share. Be open to your guidance from Spirit and be willing to surrender and allow your own transformation. Self-care and self-love are very important at these times. Be kind with you, this journey can feel daunting and messy. Rest assured that others are along this path with you even though you may feel lonely.

Yes, being an Essential is challenging and not for the faint of heart. You will be on the ride and it is best to say Yes! and work toward living in the flow as much as possible. Know that the Universe unfolds for personal good as well as the that of the Universe. It is only when we resist because of our limitations and ignorance that we create additional suffering. Keep saying Yes! Be willing to move through the cleansing fire and onto your personal path.

What's mine to do?

This question is central to the mission and actions of an Essential. Always begin with this question in some form. *What is mine to do, really?* The more empathic you are, the more likely you are to take on others' energy and think it is yours. Knowing what is for you to do can help you discern what the next best action is.

Each morning, take some quiet time and ask: *What is mine to do?* Then listen to your heart. You will have a feeling or a hunch or hear some sort of words or direction (not audibly, rather from your inner knowing). Use your Essential Variation and new awareness to discern your deeper response to the question.

CHAPTER 8

As you listen, allow any fears or resistance to be released. Sweep them away gently, like sweeping a cobweb from the corner of your room. Allow the message to emerge about *what is yours to do* even more clearly. Simply sit and see. Experience the message and your guidance.

When the resistance and fears subside, shift your attention to all the possibilities that are available to you. In quiet and stillness, allow your mind to become even more open. Know that all the possibilities are ever-present, and many are beyond your current consciousness. You may want to journal some of your insights and the information you are receiving.

Remember, if you are wondering what the next step looks like, take your next best action. Take a step and see what feedback you receive. Take a step and if it is not into life, wholeness, and healing, you'll know. You will get the message spiritually first and then physically. The acknowledgement of Spirit leading and guiding you is the belief that you are not all alone here on Earth. This connection guides you. When you know that you are living in a supportive Universe, you also know that you will get messages when you are off base. You can then choose another path, without judgement or blame. You will also get messages and indications when you are on track. By being open and receptive, you can navigate your personal mission with much more ease.

The world is alive with glory and enchantment. The Divine or Source Energy is present everywhere. You are the light in a modern world that has been so steeped in reductionism. People aren't typically taught a more integrated and holistic view of the Universe. You are bringing to the world the deep-seated trust in the Divine by stepping into your calling as an Essential. It is time to go and do things, take action, take a stand, get going! Be fully empowered and walk in humility, being open to your own inner guidance. You will know when you are off and when you are on track. The Universe always lets you know.

Ask again *What is mine to do?* Pay attention to your deeper self. Be open to the infinite possibilities. You may want to write the impressions you receive here:

_____

_____

_____

_____

Now, go about your day maintaining your inner focus while using your Essential nature.

Actively Raise Your Vibration

Being an Essential transcends religion, dogma, and popular secular belief systems. Essentials are here to herald in a more alive and vibrant, spiritually aligned, way of living, grounded in integrity, compassion, unity, and gratitude as cornerstones. Part of the Essential experience is to raise consciousness and become increasingly elevated in consciousness. Mindfulness meditation is a powerful practice to help raise your vibration.

We are energy beings and we are made up of vital energy that can be heavy and dark or light and bright. The calling in your heart that keeps inviting you onward is drawing you toward a lighter and brighter reality. As you say Yes! to the way of living that is emerging from within you, your world and others around you become much more harmonious.

You can actively raise your vibration. You can bring light to the darkness or unknown areas within or around you. Remember RAISE as your acronym for raising your vibration.

R – Remember who you are as an Essential. Always remember that there is no place where Source is not. Remember who you are as an infinite Being and remember your personal mission in alignment with your gifts. Remember your unique variation.

A – Allow yourself to surrender to the flow Universal energy and allow it to come forth through you. You *are* an Essential, remember? Allow your inherent beauty and light to emerge into the world unencumbered by doubt, fear, grief, or worry.

I – Invite the Divine influence and direction into your daily thoughts, words and actions. This requires open minded thinking and a willingness to receive inspiration and guidance. Invite inspired thoughts realizing that they will move you in ways your ego cannot predict.

S – Speak words of Truth, Kindness, Compassion, and Love. Your words create; you can choose to create beauty, peace, and harmony. May your words reflect your inner light and calling to bring about a higher vibration. Speak to your desired vision.

CHAPTER 8

E – Exercise your unique authority. Be ever vigilant to raise your vibration higher each day. This requires action on many levels and is not for the faint of heart. My first spiritual mentor once said: "Living in the light is not for wimps; it takes courage." I remember this whenever I am tempted to avoid my responsibility as an Essential. Step up, stand up and be seen! As Stephen Covey said, "Find your voice and inspire others to find theirs."

You can choose how to live by deciding to be mad or by deciding to be glad. You are the one who gives power and form to your higher guidance. You co-create your world with every thought, word and action. Every thought is a prayer and every prayer is answered. Deciding on your thoughts and your focus can enhance or distract your calling or mission.

Focus often on raising your vibration. My ongoing mantra is *I am raising my vibration*. I say this frequently when I am around anger, fear, or grief. The higher your vibration, the more ease and harmony you experience and the more you are able to share from your overflow. You know you are giving from your overflow because your inner resources energetically and otherwise remain full and what you are giving is from the extra. Think if a fountain. The overflow of water is what keep it going. If the water level drops, the fountain does not work properly and will eventually dry up if not replenished. This is the same for you. You must keep charging your own batteries as you transform and share your Essential gifts.

I think of my inner self holding a light that is bright at times and dimmer at other times. Still, over my lifetime, the light is becoming more consistently bright. Sometimes, I think of other Essentials who have gone before and learn from their journey. When I look at traditional scriptures and remind myself that *Christ* means the "enlightened one," I read the messages with fresh eyes and saw how they personally apply to me. We all have an inner light that is working to emerge and become brighter and brighter. By allowing the higher spiritual principles to be your guiding force, your light becomes even more brilliant and transformative.

Energetic Change

As your vibration elevates and you are more open to the messages and experience of being an Essential, you may feel shaky, anxious, nauseous or tingly. Sometimes, sleep may elude you or you may feel like you are getting the flu. Some Essentials experience a restlessness or unexplained angst coupled with depersonalization. This experience is called Chemicalization. Chemicalization is the physical expression of your body raising its vibration to a higher level. This is normal. You may become alarmed yet once you are able to focus on your higher vibrations, the sensations subside as your body adapts. These times can be challenging.

You may also experience other changes. Your eyesight may get better and more acute. Your experience of your emotions will become more sensitive and reflective. Your intuitive abilities expand, and you know what you did not know previously. You may notice enhanced sensory experiences.

Your body is made of energy as is everything. As you expand and elevate your vibration spiritually, the body must follow. Because the body is denser than Spirit or emotions, you may feel the movement more profoundly. It takes more energy to raise the body's vibration than to raise your awareness and understanding.

Amazing ease and a sense of lightness abounds. As your energy raises, so too does your life experience. This is a time of celebration and also a great time to connect with others who understand and have walked this road. Having another to speak with and share your experiences will help ease any fears or seeming stress. We are meant to be in community with others. Seek those who are on a similar path and your synergy will support both of you.

Ponder these questions as you become more familiar with your calling and vision. You may want to write your thoughts here.

1. Who am I?

_____
_____
_____
_____

2. Who do I say I am?

_____
_____
_____
_____

CHAPTER 8

By being able to articulate your identity on several levels, you are then able to connect to your unique Essential gifts and talents. Your words and definitions point to something much greater, yet they are necessary as a point of contact for human dialogue and connection.

Changes can yield many conflicting and confusing experiences. As an Essential, you experience intensities more profoundly than many of those around you. I encourage you to focus on transformation rather than simple change. Your experience of stepping into your spiritual calling and gift is not a simple change. You living your gift is saying yes to the Universe. In that moment, the Universe assists your journey. Yes, the journey is exciting, scary, lonely, joyful, bright, dark and intense at times, yet you are fully equipped and able to live fully expressing your gifts. Otherwise you would not have them.

Spiritual transformation can be scary for us. This is why I am here for you and why this book is available. I am often holding the high watch for those I know and work with who are in the process of awakening on deep profound levels. For me, holding the high watch means that I think of them often and visualize them transforming in wonderful ways and that I meditate on their success, thus offering energetic/spiritual support. As other Essentials were available for me as I emerged, I am here for you as you emerge in the greater expression of your Essential gifts. After all, we are all in this together!

Every dark night and wild day have been worth the amazing peace and lightness I experience today. Even in the challenging times, the light of Source illumines my path. My human self may have struggles while my inner Spirit knows the way. Herein lies my faith and focus. You can live with this harmony too!

Your relationship with the Universe is very important. You may have some old beliefs to adjust or new concepts and understanding to develop along your path. Know that you are fully supported by the Universe. Pay attention and connect as much as possible. Your actions to take and words to speak will become clear the more you allow for the powerful connection to Source.

Questions to Ponder:

What is yours to do?

What aspects can be left behind as you focus onward?

How can you raise your vibration?

Whom can be of guidance and support?

Journal your ideas and inspirations:

Chapter 9
Your Relationship and Role with the Universe

The quieter you become the more you are able to hear.
~~Rumi

All Essentials are intensely connected to the energy of the Universe. As you awaken and transcend your old beliefs and ways, you will go through several phases. These phases may move quickly at times and slowly at other times. Each Essential has a unique path. Your path, vision and mission are uniquely yours. Review these important courses of action and see what you identify with as part of your process. Keep in mind that you may be in different places in various areas of your life.

Awareness – Acknowledgment

Having awareness and paying attention to the messages are crucial for your happiness and ease of living from your Essential gifts. When you notice an inner energy change or a shift in your thinking, you are experiencing this phase. It is important to acknowledge this phase as you will experience increased awareness throughout your life.

Acknowledging what is happening and that the transformation is happening may be challenging at times. Many people have difficulty identifying who to safely share with in confidence. Be sure to acknowledge your sensations, insights and experiences.

Paying attention to your inner and outer world makes a tremendous difference as you bring your vision into reality. The more aware you become, the more effective you will be in using your gifts for good.

Try on Inspired Ideas

As you become increasingly aware of the great things emerging from deep within you, take time to try on your new vibe. Make friends with your awareness and energy-shifts. These times are inspiring and are part of your process. Sometimes you may have to adjust to the new vibe and sometimes it will feel like coming home. It is all part of the process. Practice experiencing your Essential gifts and intensities without judgment.

Trying on elevated levels of consciousness and energy will help you ease into your future. It is when you resist growing and developing that you can cause anger, strife, or frustration in your relationships. Your inspired ideas are just that, inspired. They are meant for you to test them and see how they resonate with your vision. See how your Essential variations add depth to your inspirations.

Trying on these ideas is much like trying on clothes. Some fit right away and you love them. Others take some time to get used to and then you grow into the new style. Others simply do not it at this moment. The ones that do not fit may be something to remember for a future time. Always make a practice of trying on inspired ideas and new awareness.

Practicing

As your awareness grows and you become more comfortable with your talents, practice using your gifts more frequently. Practice honoring and following your impressions. Sometimes you may be compelled to share something with another or give something to another. Following your guided impressions builds confidence.

Your confidence grows with confirmation of the message. This way you are poising yourself to receive more blessings and awareness to support your mission and growth. Note that each Essential variation may receive and grow differently. There is no one way, there is only your way.

I find that practicing my new behaviors or paradigms is helpful because it generates consistency and a new, stronger foundation. Rehearsing the new creates a new history from which to act. This is valuable when your emotions are intense or running high for any reason. When you have emotional intensity happening, your logical brain may not be as accessible so you will naturally revert to what your system knows. You want it to be the most effective so practicing the skills and awareness pays off.

No one is expected to learn things in solitude or secret then emerge with all knowledge. Oldest and only children may have the old belief that they do not have the right to make mistakes and practice, yet you do! We learn best when practicing and receiving feedback. You may even seem to fail or fall short. Pay attention to your lessons learned as they will always come in handy at some point in the future.

Timing

Spiritual unfoldment can vary greatly from physical reality. There is a physical timing that must be considered by all Essentials. The population is waking up, some much slower than others. These shifts and changes can be tiring and challenging as well as exhilarating. Often, there is a time lag between your spiritual or inner awareness and the physical reality. This time varies from seconds to maybe even years. Timing is impacted by others, the collective and your own awareness and vibration.

The more you allow your Essential gifts to emerge and become apparent, the easier timing will be day to day. Each Essential variation has different relationships with time and added gifts like being and empath or indigo or intuitive can impact timing as well. Where Workers and Ballers may use time for productivity and measure their success this way, Creators, Weavers and Harmonizers may use progress along creative or spiritual lines as the measure of productivity. Keep in mind that time and timing impact each of us differently. Do not assume others experience time in the same or similar manner that you do.

Sometimes when you are trying on and practicing new paradigms or beliefs, you may feel lopsided. Maybe your intellect will be overactive or underactive. Maybe your spiritual connection becomes heightened and thus you make changes. Regardless, as an Essential, you are meant to be a leader in elevating consciousness in the way that aligns with you. This is where being curious can be a real asset.

For example, I have a client who engages in deep spiritual practices and has for years. He will often state that he receives spiritual/intuitive guidance about his life and career. He also states that sometimes it takes a little time for his rational or intellectual mind to be able to fully understand the meaning of spiritual message. He shares with me that he is always amazed as he watches the outcome of his insights. Your personal timing is moderated by your openness and willingness to go deep within and allow your core essence to show up. From this place you can use your Essential gifts in making a noise that is beneficial for all.

Zone of Proximal Development

If you bring too bright a light or too high a vibration to a situation, it could actually work against you. The zone of proximal development is the zone in which a person can grow and stretch without causing a healing crisis.

Every person has a zone of proximal development for all things new. Pushing this zone too far too fast causes a disconnection and often some sort of crisis that then devolves into a negative situation.

As an Essential, you experience life differently than many others. It is vital to be aware of this and to speak to and engage with others where they are and move them along as they request in a way in which their timing is considered. Someone who is desperate for change will have different timing than someone who is not desperate.

As you grow or work with others, remembering this zone will help you be more effective and less frustrated. Every person has their comfort zone for learning and trying new things. Some people are more open and available to take risks in growth areas. Some folks are slower to try new things. There is no wrong way, yet as an Essential, you are often leading the way. Pay attention to the feedback you are receiving to discern your pace.

Our goal as Essentials is to be the light in the physical world. It is not our light; it is Universal Light. Know that you and others will get it and start transforming when ready. You are here to shine brightly without being distracted by others' responses or their paths. Your Essential gifts are meant to be brought into the open.

Releasing the Outdated

The old and outdated must leave for the new to emerge. This includes beliefs, ideas, words, actions, relationships, and paradigms. In a world where people are holding on to so much, this part of living the Essential life can be challenging. Essential falling apart is when you disintegrate the old way so that a new way can be envisioned, created, established, and grown. It can feel much like being consumed by the fire of trials and eventually emerging like a phoenix. There can be no phoenix without a fire. Fires are cleansing and needed for your growth. As things that are no longer needed disintegrate, practice allowing your human experience alongside your spiritual experience. Your experience becomes a yes/and rather than an either/or. This makes your personal transformation more inclusive and less difficult.

Being an Essential does not mean it is OK to act in self-centered unenlightened ways – all in the name of being an Essential. To be an Essential means that you are responsible for acknowledging and developing your skills and gifts in ways that serve the greater Good. To deny your light is to hide on many levels. Your responsibility is to use your abilities, gifts and variation for the benefit and good, not to control or manipulate.

You are in this world and not of this world. Thus, you are called to live in and master both worlds, the seen and the unseen. You have the skill set and ability to accomplish this way of living. The light and the power can be very seductive, yet the 3D reality is also very important. Going through a time where you want to remain in the higher vibe without bringing it to your day to day human life happens to everyone from time to time, yet this is not a good idea in the long run.

Better to see how you use your spiritual skills and gifts while also tending to your earthly responsibilities. These things are not mutually exclusive. You are both spiritual and physical so both must be considered when transforming and bringing your gifts forth.

Disruption, Trauma, Stress, and Change

When you are experiencing deep pain, trauma, or loss, allow your full experience of these emotions within your personal healing zone. Even if you feel broken, let yourself feel it fully in a safe way. In this place, in that feeling, is the birthplace of a new you, a new way and new level of health you have not previously known. By being open and curious, you do not become bitter and act in an unhealthy manner. You are to be the light for the others. Choose to be ever expanding just as the Universe is ever expanding.

Yes, birth and growth can be messy and frustrating. After all, you are an Essential, not a camp counselor. Take time apart to think about your beliefs, your ideas, your responses, and your choices. Give yourself permission to improve or shift things as you are led. You are continuously unfolding. Allowing serves better than fighting and resisting.

Within stress and disruption is an amazing invitation. Even when you cannot immediately see it, the invitation exists. Your personal invitation is from the Divine, inviting you to choose to become more awake and evolve your consciousness rather than become bitter because of the wound. If you do not say yes to the invitation, you become angry, hostile and bitter. You lower your vibration and decrease your own inner light. Because you have free will, you may choose this way. I find this way has much suffering. Still, you are in charge and can choose whatever road you wish.

I have worked with many Essentials over the years who became bitter and angry and faded away into depression. Their worlds became dark because they chose bitterness over the invitation to experience conscious growth. Some Essentials choose loneliness and disconnection, which builds a formidable wall around their heart and gut, thus creating marked inner pain and discord. Sadly, many Essentials stop there and cheat themselves of a rich and vibrant life. If you feel disconnected, please, please seek some assistance and be willing to dive deep within and clean out the mess that has been accumulating for decades. Cleaning your vessel from the inside-out has great payoffs which include decreased physical pain, much improved authentic relationships and more. Please, when you experience a disruption in your life, look for the invitation and say Yes! to Source. This will serve you, your community, and the world.

Begin to look deeper into events and challenges. Look for the deeper causes of the effect you are experiencing. Begin to ask new questions and seek new answers by being curious and open. As you move beyond the story, you become free and able to bring your light to the service of others. You will experience compassion and a beautiful diversity within and all around.

How Essentials Grow and Evolve

Always keep in mind that your growth and transformation are seasonal. I like to think of this like the seasons in nature. By following a seasonal type of growth, you are now empowered to have compassion for you and others. Transformation is not a linear process. Linear would be the thinking that "if I have been doing this personal growth life for 1 year, then I should be in a certain place". Expecting that the time, progress continuum is predictable along a straight line is not how our transformation happens. Rather it is along more of a circular path that also is moving forward and upward in direction. Let's look at the seasonal way of approaching your growth and transformation.

Winter is the time of darkness and deep rest. By going within and resting deeply, you can build energy and resources for the new ideas and visions that you are called to create. Winter is the rest following a time of hard work and creation. This rest is also akin to taking a sabbath or rest following any shorter period of work. Seasonally, this means that one quarter of your time devoted to a project or overall transformation is devoted to deep, nurturing rest.

Many Essentials may struggle with this if they are following the belief that they always need to be creating and pushing or moving forward. You are not a machine; you are in a human body and the body must have down time to rest and replenish on deep cellular levels.

Spring follows winter in the seasons. Spring is the time of renewal and new growth. During this season, your new and expansive ideas and visions begin to sprout into reality. Seeds are planted so the new can begin to take root. Much like a new plant shoot, these new ideas and visions are tender and require love, compassion and tenderness for their optimal development. Being too harsh or trying to force their development may yield in a crisis or even the death of the new idea or project.

Essentials may want to hurry things along, or even try to "help" the timing, yet the power of the seasons is more powerful that all your amazing ideas and contrived plans. It is best to allow the flow of the season to assist your timing and growth. Not all things can be accomplished in a day or even a weekend. Sometimes what you are growing may be years in this springtime of new growth.

Summer is the goring season. Plenty of sunshine and rain to help your idea and transformation flourish. Too dry looks like multiple distractions and taking your focus off of the newly growing vision. Too wet looks like being overly protective and overdoing things to the point where you literally drown the new vision. The Sunshine is the love, Universal energy and Gratitude that you shine onto your own vision and transformation.

The Summer growing season is often well received by Essentials because you can see things changing and expanding. This is familiar and desired by many Essentials. Some Essentials may think the summer season is too hot and may shelter the new growth and thus stop the vital nutrients from being assimilated. Summer can be a great balance and fertile season. If you are an Essential who is resisting your growth, you may struggle when being invited to grow. This could be a place to receive added support.

Fall is the season to harvest all the rewards of your growing season. This I a powerful and rewarding time. When you have worked all summer to grow, the harvest is the beginning of a slowing down and preparation for the upcoming winter of rest. Reaping your harvest may be a challenge depending upon your belief system Many Essentials that I have worked with over the years, had a difficult time at first receiving the reward of their labor. They often reported that they did not think they deserved it or that someone else could benefit more.

WHERE DO YOU FIT IN?

You deserve to receive the bounty of your harvest that comes as a result of your growth. Your inner growth and transformation are meant for you to then create the new seed energy that you will then develop during the winter and plant in the early spring. The cycle is inherently perfect and on time; never early and never late. Trust in the elegant simplicity of the Universe and of your personal Essential variation is required to take full advantage of this season as you enter the winter season once again.

Winter is the season of rest and creating the seeds internally that will be planted and brought forth. Thus, the circular or seasonal way is much more conducive to being effective in support of your Essential gifts and transformation.

What is your favorite season? Explain.

_____
_____
_____
_____

What is your most difficult season? Explain.

_____
_____
_____
_____

How can you use the seasons to foster healthy transformation in an area of your life?

_____
_____
_____
_____
_____
_____

Meet Maggie Mae

Maggie Mae is a Creator Essential with many Weaver characteristics. Maggie Mae loves to create, and she focuses easily on her creations which speaks to some Worker Essential variation as well. Maggie Mae is an author and she loves to create using the written word. We met when she called and scheduled a consult to look at her heart's desire and how to become unstuck and move forward. Maggie Mae was wise beyond her 30 years of age and she had great insight.

Early in Maggie Mae's life she would think of herself as a machine and she would say she could push through any deadline to get the job done. Maggie Mae prided herself on her drive. It was not long, and Maggie Mae was burned out and she shared in a session with me that she just gave up. She was exhausted and discouraged. Maggie Mae had so many amazing ideas of things to write about that she did not focus and therefore nothing was written as she would have liked. I explained to Maggie Mae that she was following a linear type of work logic that is not friendly to people in general and particularly Essentials.

With some focus and desire to make the inner paradigm changes Maggie Mae started to live in a more seasonal manner. She started with winter and took time off to rest, have some deep inner reflection and to envision her possibilities. When she felt rested and rejuvenated, Maggie Mae began to feel the call to write naturally. She told me in a session that she woke up one day and the creative itch was there, so she began to write. She realized while she was writing that morning that the content was profound and that she could never have gone to that level the way she was working.

We also discussed having an internal locus of control rather than an external locus of control. Maggie Mae's external locus of control means that she focused outside of herself for validation and to know what to do and when. She was reacting to the world around her. An internal locus of control means that you are acting upon the world from the inside out. This is very different that being reacting to outside people and events constantly. Maggie Mae began to learn the difference and focus on her internal locus of control She was able to become more focused, self-assured and peaceful.

With some focused mentoring and ongoing support, Maggie Mae was able to create and grow her vision, receive the harvest and reward and then give herself permission to rest before moving onto the next project. Her timing was not that of the physical seasons. What is important is that she honored the seasons of her personal process. This more circular approach to your Essential gifts yields more powerful transformation.

Questions to Ponder:

What is your understanding and experience of your relationship with the Universe?

What is your understanding and experience of your role in the Universe?

How does timing impact your inspirations coming into reality?

What effective ways do you handle change?

How do you know that you are willing to make changes to release disconnection?

How can you apply the seasons to your Essential expression?

How are you honoring the seasons of your life?

Journal your ideas and inspirations:

Chapter 10
Your Expansion and Transformation

I will whisper secrets in your ear, just nod yes and be silent.
~~Rumi

As you grow and evolve, you become new each day. Spiritual growth means that you transcend your previous ways of seeing and include new ideas, thoughts, words and actions as you expand. You are not leaving all of you behind and starting over, though it feels that way at times. Part of your calling is to remember that you expand with a *yes/and* map. You will inherently take with you to your next chapter what is needed, and you must then allow for the release of what is not needed for the next chapter so the new can emerge in that space. This is quite miraculous, really.

You transcend your old ways and your vibration is elevated and your consciousness expanded, and you become more awake! You include new ideas and ways of seeing yourself, your community, the world and the Divine. You don't actually leave yourself; you include what came before and needs to be brought forth while you are willing to release what no longer serves.

When you hold on to the old way and cut yourself off from new, transforming ideas, you run the risk of narcissism or becoming stuck. Holding on to and defending something at the expense of your peace of mind is a form of right-fighting. When you must be right rather than happy, this is a great time to seek counsel and make some inner changes. Right fighting is a sign that you are holding onto an old belief or paradigm. The more you hold on, the more disconnected from your inner Source you become. This is ineffective at best. At worst, you end up developing additional challenges to address, like severed relationships, that will not serve you.

The Universe is ever expanding, and we are part of this glorious expansion. As you connect to your personal expansion, you also become aware of your community and eventually the world. Some Essentials spend more time in any one of these following areas and as it serves, it is useful and helpful.

Allow Emergence from Within

There is freedom in allowing. Allowing the messages and energies to move through you and into the physical reality, you may be tempted to want to stop your transformative process. This can happen if you feel afraid or unsure. Take time to speak with others along the transformative road and share. You will quickly notice that some of the unconscious resistance is more common that you think. It is not something to be afraid of, rather it is something to embrace and move through. Resistance simply yields discontent and an ongoing yearning and searching. It is much easier and better to allow the Universe to move through you than to resist and create dis-ease.

To allow means to release fears and resistance. This is when you have the opportunity to move forward as Universal energy moves through you. It can come in the form of inspired ideas or premonitions or prophetic dreams. When it is your time to awaken, nothing human can stop the power of the Universe. My best advice is to allow the emergence and surround yourself with trusted others who have walked this path of transformation and transcendence.

The sense of community and connection is required for your success and satisfaction. There is a sense of safety and comfort that is born of an understanding support system. It may feel tempting at times to withdraw. I encourage you to seek safe and understanding people to create your connections.

Say YES! to your inner calling and heart's desire. Say YES! to the calling of the Universe and your role in bringing expansion and transformation. By allowing, you are free. Free to evolve and be the Essential that you are meant to be here and now.

Curious Questions and Statements

When things are happening, and you do not know what to do or where to turn, it helps to use curious questions to help focus your thinking and emotions. Curious questions lead your inner thoughts and the responses of others into productive territory. Curious statements that I use include: "Help me understand" and "Tell me more". These are open ended and allow for improved information, connection, and understanding.

When experiencing sensations, downloads (inspired messages) or emotions that are intense, your best responses could be "wow", "interesting," or "fascinating". Attempting to focus on the "Why" questions can cause static and inner conflict. Simply noticing without judgment is the most powerful response. Do not try to change things, simply observe your experience and document ideas and connections if you are led to do so. Know that all energy changes over time so even when you feel like you are stuck, you are not stuck unless you hold on to something old. Energy moves in waves and thus is always changing.

Be curious, open the "how" doors which offers you some potential answers to your dilemmas. By adopting the beginner's mind with a level of curiosity and innocence, you will gain great awareness and direction. The beginner's mind is the mindset of someone who is new to a particular idea or behavior. Understanding that a seasoned mind can get stuck in a rut, the beginner is always learning, thus approaches tasks and ideas differently that the expert. This is far superior to having to know "why". As Buddha said, "Why Not?". Knowing why something is happening tells us why but it does not help with actual strategy or direction of action or thought. When you hear yourself asking a "why" question, ask yourself "How will knowing why help?" Typically, outside of satisfying intellectual banter, why is not effective.

Discernment

Discernment is a very important skill to develop for all Essentials. For some, this skill may come easier than for others. Discernment and judgment are similar yet quite different in one important detail. I notice many Essentials interchanging these words so I would like to take a moment a differentiate judgment and discernment.

Judgment is when you assess a person, situation or opportunity and then assign value. For example: "This person gives me the creeps, so they are a bad person" or "That person is not as sensitive as me, so I am better than them" or "This party is boring to me, so it is a bad event." In all these statements, value is being assigned. This is judgment.

Discernment is when you notice whether something resonates with you or not and then make a decision about your actions based on your inner experience *without* assigning value. For example: "This person gives me the creeps, I think I will speak with someone else" or "This is interesting, that person is not as sensitive as me." or "This party is boring to me, how can I add some enthusiasm?" In all these statements, the person is using discernment *without* assigning value.

Essential gifts are meant to emerge through you to enhance and bring to life your world in an uplifting manner. Taking advantage of your Essential variation is part of your ongoing discernment practice. Determining how to use your Essential gift in a discerning manner is exciting and empowering. There is a learning curve and it is most helpful to have others of like mind assisting you are you develop your discernment skills.

Meet Samantha

Samantha is able to "know" what is going on in others' lives. She has the ability to read their energy and have an understanding of what they are going through. Samantha has Baller Essential variation. Samantha has had to learn what to say when for the benefit of others. Samantha has shared that as a young girl she would use her skills to manipulate her parents and then peers. Samantha was well adept at controlling others and manipulating situations for her selfish motives when we met. She had a basic idea of what she was doing, and she thought she had some kind of mental illness. After all, she was acting like someone with a personality disorder. As we uncovered her motives, fears, gifts and life events, the unfolding of her challenges became obvious.

Samantha learned to identify her gifts and focus her energy toward beneficial efforts for others concerned. She became a shining light in the lives of her friends, co-workers and family as she was able to see what was happening under the surface and then use her impressions for compassionate and supportive responses and interactions. Samantha is now enjoying authentic and deeper quality relationships as a result of using her gift for the greater Good.

There are some great questions to ponder that will assist you in your connection and help you deepen your ability to listen to your inner voice that is inviting you forward. Take some time and answer these questions. There are no right or wrong answers, there is simply how you answer today. Always reserve the right to change your mind and remember that as you grow, your answers will naturally change to align with your ever-raising vibration.

CHAPTER 10

1. How shall I practice gratitude?

2. How shall I practice acceptance?

3. How shall I practice simplicity?

4. How shall I practice flow?

5. How then shall I live?

By pondering deeper questions and determining how you would live according to these principles, you become an even brighter and more illuminated instrument. It is in these moments that you are truly offering your gift with humility and grace. As you awaken and transform, you will experience these on varied levels.

Expanding Consciousness

You are always growing, even on the days that seem dark or confusing. As an Essential, you are uniquely called to bring into reality a higher consciousness in daily practice. Your growth and curiosity mean that you will soon leave your old ways behind and move in faith into a new way with a new community surrounding you. This does not mean that anyone is right or wrong. Every person has their unique calling and it is vital that we allow our inner calling to emerge. As Essentials, we are charged with inspiring others and assisting in bringing others into greater light.

To do this work, you must be consistently growing and stretching your own consciousness. Surround yourself with a community of like-minded Essentials, no matter what they call themselves. While being sure to connect with your community, be sure also to take time daily to connect within, with your own inner essence. If you spend too much of your energy on others without caring for your own flame, you will soon burn out. This is why there are so many episodes of psychological stress and dysfunction including burnout, compassion fatigue and adrenal fatigue among creatives and healers. When you over-give because you are compelled to serve, and you are not taking excellent care of your own resources, compassion fatigue and burnout become an unfortunate reality.

Take time for you and allow yourself to be renewed regularly. To walk in the fullness of grace and blessings, put yourself in position by caring for you in authentic ways. Always begin with your own personal path including prayer and meditation and connection with nature. Without first filling your resources, it is impossible to truly give. When you are filled within, then give from your personal overflow. In this way, everyone wins!

Chapter 11
Faith in Action

Faith in action is Love and Love in action is service.
~~Mother Teresa

As an Essential, your faith is the fuel that continues to move you along your road of expansion. As you unfold and evolve, you then offer connection and support in powerful ways. Faith is the invisible substance of your heart's desire and vision. It is only when we take focused action that springs from an inner knowing or faith that we, as Essentials, enjoy the wonder of our authentic gifts.

Putting your faith and calling as an Essential into action is making noise. Your noise may be physically quieter than another, yet it is noise, all the same. Your noise may be leading or serving others in any number of ways. Your noise may be as an activist, author, poet, musician, or educator. Mother Teresa made noise by taking her mission seriously and following through, regardless of what anyone else thought or said. She trusted her connection and she allowed her unique Essential mission to come through.

Here are some unique considerations as you open up and grow into a full expression of your Essential gifts.

Unique Qualification

You are uniquely qualified to bring forth your personal calling and mission. Each Essential has a unique, personal mission. Some may seem similar, yet we are all here with a unique purpose and calling. You will also bring forth your calling in your personal and connected way. Your human flair and creativity in fulfilling your vision is of great value. Free will includes how you respond to your inner guidance. You are here on purpose with a purpose and only you can fulfill your personal mission. This is exciting and can also be daunting at times. If it wasn't meant for you to do, you would not be thinking about it. Thus, your success is assured.

You know your calling because it won't leave you alone. The ideas and opportunities just keep coming, even when you try to distract yourself or stop all together. If it is part of your Essential mission, you will be reminded if you are distracted or get off course. You alone possess what you alone are called to do. Faith in action means that you say "YES" and follow your personal higher guidance. You will know if your inner prompting and messages are Divine guidance because the guidance will be for the good of all concerned.

Acceptance

Acceptance is the answer to all your challenges, struggles and disruptions. Acceptance means you are in the flow and allowing yourself to live moment to moment. You know you are experiencing acceptance when you can acknowledge a circumstance and you are able to be with it at face value without judgment or running away.

Acceptance takes practice. You may not feel accepting at times. It is OK to have your ups and downs. No one is always accepting of everything. Acceptance is not the same as agreement. You can accept some situation or event or person and not be in agreement at the same time.

Acceptance becomes more of a spiritual practice the more you breathe and live in the moment. Acceptance is more about being in flow and releasing attachments that are detrimental to your well-being. The function of acceptance is energy conservation. When you are living in a state of acceptance you are able to use less energy because of less resistance and distractions.

Be Quiet and Breathe

Inner quiet is essential for Essentials. To be the transforming agent that you are meant to be, inner quiet is where your inspiration and guidance enters your consciousness. When it is noisy within your mind and emotions, you are not able to properly hear the messages the Universe is attempting to share with you.

As with quiet, breathing is essential. Real, full, diaphragmatic breaths are required for authentic connection and satisfaction. Your messages are coming through and you will be able to receive them when you are breathing properly. Exhale any stress, tension or low energy and inhale light, joy and peace. Consistently breathing and allowing your lungs to receive the oxygen. Healthy Breathing is an important part of being an Essential.

Holding your breath means that you are not getting enough oxygen which causes anxiety, distractions, and foggy thinking. When you are holding your breath, it often means that you are holding on to some sort of subconscious pain or separation. Holding your breath is a signal to breathe deeply, identify, accept then release the pain (separation) that is clouding your system.

As you breathe fully and open to higher consciousness, you will see expanded possibilities. From this place, you grow and evolve to higher levels of awareness and service. This is the Essential journey.

Learning to establish and maintain inner quiet takes time and dedication. Breathing full breaths can elude you when you are hurried or stressed. This is a meaningful intersection of your old paradigm and the new one where connection is mandatory. When you slow the pace and refuse to run yourself into the ground, your entire life changes. It all starts and proceeds with the breath!

Connection is the Correction

It is essential that you are connected. Your faith requires that you are connected to your Source, which presents as the Spirit within, the Spirit in others and the Spirit of the Universe. These connections work to correct disruption and misunderstandings. Connection is the healing power that comes from allowing the Spirit within you to be an active part of your daily life. The more you trust your Source energy within, the more connected you become and the more your unique gifts emerge. This is the goal.

As humans, we are required to be in connection with others of the same species because humans are pack animals and personal connection is required to thrive. Connecting within to your personal inner guidance and higher self is an ongoing practice that is also required for your happiness and satisfaction. If you do not already have one, create daily, protected time for going within and listening. Simply listen to your inner voice. This daily practice will make your journey much friendlier to your system. Sometimes the shifts can be difficult so going within every day is most important to help you breathe through the tough spots.

Remember that you came from the Divine and everything comes from the same source. Essentials allow themselves to be lived by this greater source without attempting to take over and let cognitive, egoistic thinking take over.

Be Open. Be Receptive.

Be open to your life experiences. You are the cause of the effects in your life. What is happening is a great feedback loop to show you where in your conscious and unconscious areas any trip points are hiding. Maybe you can see a particular pattern repeating itself. Look for the unconscious or conscious beliefs, attitudes, thoughts and words that support the repeating effects. If you wish to release the effect, then you must go within, identify the inner cause and be willing to replace and transform your own belief system and paradigm.

Being open to the messages and guidance is vital in your growth. When your ego attempts to take control and your self-will shuts down your receptiveness to higher ideals, you are setting yourself up for a challenging time and possibly resentments and anger.

Being receptive means to pay attention. I always say: "Head's up!" Paying attention and receiving your deep, inner guidance and intuitions will support your journey. Be open and receptive so that you can respond based on the highest good.

Are you willing and able to receive the good life that is yours by your birthright? Many Essentials start with an underlying sense of unworthiness and grief. This can make receiving your good life challenging. You are here to be a beneficial presence and you have a right to be here. Be open to your guidance for it is uniquely yours. Respond to your guidance in ways that align with the highest good for all.

Redirect as Needed

As your essential gifts rise to the surface and become more apparent. Your intellectual or thinking mind may fight back and try to keep you in bondage to what once was. Your body and soul are intrinsically linked, and they will keep expanding and moving forward with much more ease than your mind at times.

In this heavily weighted intellectual world, you may have challenges releasing the old patterns and templates from which you lived your life. As your authentic Essential nature emerges and develops, you transform from the inside out. Your brain may not want to handle this well.

Realize that as you live from your Essential nature, you will be releasing old patterns and ways of seeing the world and evolving into a more transformative lifestyle. The most effective way to help your brain along is to catch the old patterns that are causing discord and then redirect your thinking to the new, updated paradigm as soon you notice the old slipping into your mind. Because the Universe is always expanding, your paradigms must, by definition, continue to expand.

Trying to hold onto old ideas and ways of being will thwart your Essential gifts from merging and supporting the unity-based consciousness that is unfolding from within. Redirect your thinking as often as you catch your thinking stuck on old ideas or outdated concepts. Continue to learn and seek higher ways to express your essential gifts.

Your brain may be stubborn but remember that you are the thinker behind your thoughts, and you do have control and authority to make any change you desire. It may take more focus and effort than you think, and it is still completely attainable.

The Art of Nonattachment

Practice letting go of your need to control outcomes, people, or events. The truth is that everything will be just fine, and you are not here to control. Control comes from fear. Fear clouds and disrupts faith. Thus, control is not a viable choice for Essentials.

Nonattachment means that you are fully involved in your work and calling while not being attached to the outcome. You have a knowingness that the outcome will be perfect and attaching to an outcome only causes problems. Nonattachment and detachment are very different. Detachment means that you do not care about what is happening or care about engaging at all. Nonattachment means that you care deeply yet you are not holding onto agenda for the outcome. Nonattachment is the best road of the Essential.

Your best idea today is tapping only a small percentage of possibilities. One little change and things are open further, and your possibilities expand. Being nonattached to outcome allows you flexibility in how and when you respond to life events or demands of others.

Ceremony

A ceremony is a ritual observance that happens in formal and notable occasions. Ceremonies are an important part of growth and transformation. Essentials create and participate in ceremonies that honor their journey and the journey of others. I am often called upon to help create ceremony for Essentials and others who are emerging into a more dynamic spiritual lifestyle.

Reflect on your personal life and spiritual practices for a minute. Some ceremonies are more formal, like a wedding, baptism or christening, graduation or celebration of life. These document major and significant life transitions and milestones. Some ceremonies are informal and often intimate, like a birthday, anniversary, house blessing or personal milestone. Still the ceremony is a vital part of your transcendence and acknowledgment of your road.

What are the milestones and happenings that you wish to preserve with ceremony? What are your ceremonies? Do you have ceremony around holidays or special events? These opportunities offer vital and valuable connection with others in your sphere of influence.

As an Essential, the ceremonies have special significance and value. When you acknowledge others with ceremony, you are honoring them and you. When you come forth, leading a ceremony with your Essential gifts shining brightly, everyone is transformed whether they know it right away or not. Notice the ceremonies you create in your daily life and notice how they support our growth and transformation.

What are your personal ceremonies?

_____
_____
_____
_____
_____
_____
_____

Are there any ceremonies you wish to create?

_____

_____

_____

_____

Employ Patience

Sometimes the 3-dimensional aspects of life can be very challenging and difficult. Many Essentials prefer a higher, more enlightened way of being. Essentials are by definition ahead of their time and are here on Earth to bring in the light or powerful transformation. If your road seems difficult and even hard, patience and observing can be a real help.

It takes time for your spiritual awareness and knowingness to drop into physical 3-dimenional form in time and space. From an inspired idea to fruition for me is about 18 months to 2 years most of the time. There are also times when the manifestation is much faster. Part of my Essential gifts is my connection with my deeper self and receiving understanding that takes some time to actually appear in my life. Once, I was writing in my journal and a new friend and how I was interested in our conversation about existential ideas. All of a sudden, I started thinking about how our friendship would develop and that he would be tapping into my knowledge which will help in a much larger way that I could see. About 21 months later, my friend shared with me that he used some of my ideas in a business plan for his company and it blew the doors off their projections. He also said he did not know why he started sharing it when he did, but he was glad he did share. Because I allowed my Essential gift to come out and be seen, the benefit was greater than I could see. Having patience in seeing how your Essential gift will emerge and be seen is a great virtue.

I have had to develop patience over the years and at times this is quite a challenge. Being able to slow down and breathe and go with the flow around you can be an excellent way to use patience in your favor.

Live with Intention

The Creator variation feels at home here. When you live purposefully with focus, your daily life becomes even more magical and inspiring. To live with intention is a mental discipline that then leads to emotional and physical discipline. This discipline yields awe inspiring spiritual experiences and unfolding possibilities for you and your mission. There are 4 primary ways to bring about your Essential vision with intention. They are to live out loud, learn humbly, love soulfully, and lead boldly. Let's look at these ideas briefly.

Live Out Loud means to live with passion on purpose and with intention. The Harmonizer variation is at home here. Allow inner passion for life and living to take your breath away with awe and wonder. Have you fully lived the last 2,000 days or have you lived that same day 2,000 times? Asking this question helps you awake from your walking trance and brings focus to the very day you are living *today*. Live each day with passion and compassion emerging through your being. This way of living is the opposite of going through the motions. You have a moment by moment choice to live in the moment full of awe and reverence or to sleepwalk, going through the motions and missing the beauty that is all around and within you. The idea of playing it safe is often an illusion. When you live with passion and are committed to experiencing life, the idea of safety and security are relative. I say, follow your passions in a focused and purposeful manner. By following your inner guidance, you are on the right track.

Learn Humbly means to be of service. The Worker Variation is at home here. Being a service-oriented leader as you grow and evolve. You learn humbly from blockages, challenges and mis-takes that you make and have made. To be humble as you learn, open your inner mental gates so that valuable information and insights can emerge. Any addiction you have to being busy can fool you into distraction and putting off your vital inner spiritual connection development. Remember that your life is a magnificent journey and every challenge, and every joy is woven into your perfect amazing tapestry. Who are you meant to be and live on your soul's path? Be aware of releasing attachment to outcome and any sense of inner pride that excludes your connection to the Divine. Being humble depends on your Universal connection while being prideful focuses on you, independent of your soul connection. Release the "I can do it myself" way of being and thinking. A simple reminder prayer could be: *"Love _____ through me the way they need to be loved and love me* *through _____ the way I need to be loved."* This type of heart-to-heart prayer takes out the ego and any false beliefs, allowing only love to be shared. All people have challenges, you are not alone.

Love Soulfully by investing your life in loving relationships with all beings. The Weaver variation is at home here. Let love be your guiding motivation in your thoughts, words and actions. Love in this setting means: "To allow another to do what is right for themselves without any insistence they satisfy you." Your ultimate success lies in answering this question: "Do you love?" How would you live today if Love was your only inner compass?

Lead Boldly as you resolutely awaken and move forward in your personal transcendence. The Baller variation is at home here. Be willing to share with others to inspire them to also transform. You are here to move forward, to lead, and inherently you are made for more. By leading boldly, you open doors for you and others using your connection to the higher principles of the Universe of Love, gratitude, kindness and compassion. Seek the high road on purpose. You are here in this time and space to leave a legacy so teach and share what you know and are learning; it is the way to immortality. Pleasing others while ignoring or marginalizing your own self-care is the one thing that stops you from being the bold leader you are meant to be. Always be authentic and you will be living your personal, unique spiritual imprint! What is most important is between you and the Divine. Live the life made for you in all ways always.

Questions to Ponder:

In what ways are you open and receptive?

How do you use ceremony to support your expansion?

What are some ways you can add stillness and breathe to your daily life?

What are your personal intentions for the next 2 years?

Journal your ideas and inspirations:

Chapter 12
Health Challenges Caused by Avoidance and Denial

Knowing your own darkness is the best method for dealing with the darkness of other people.
~~Carl Jung

Many Essentials resist the energy and inspired ideas that are emerging. Sometimes this avoidance or denial can be experienced in the form of distractions, anxiety, depression, insomnia, grief, worry, doubt, and procrastination and overwhelm. The more you ignore or repress the emerging energy, the more taxed your physical body becomes. Your body bears the burden. Every ache, pain, tension or struggle is connected to a spiritual idea, energy or concept that you are either consciously or unconsciously avoiding or ignoring.

Why do we do this? Well, look at the culture for the answer. We are trained to be specialists in intellectual or productive pursuits. For generations, responding to a higher calling or your inner vision was unacceptable and often considered deviant. Normal people did not speak of nor have time to discuss or pursue these inner promptings as they were too busy with daily tasks. Increasingly, over the past decades, uncovering and following your inner calling has become more accepted and even admired at times. When your inner vision is blocked, you will experience discomfort. This discomfort eventually leads to dis-ease if left ignored.

Ambition and focusing on achievement alone can cause challenges in your life from disconnection to health issues. When you trust things outside yourself and are not paying attention within you are living by ambition as a way of living.

You are living from ambition when you think or say things like: "I am what I have" or "I am what I do". So many Essentials go through the pain of waking out of this cultural trance saying that there is something more. Another way to tell if you are too focused outside yourself is when you feel separate from others and there is something missing in your life. This sense of disconnection is a result of and blocks your connection to your inner light.

Anxiety

Anxiety is often misdiagnosed as a mental health concern and then promptly medicated in keeping with traditional Western medicine. I find that anxiety is a great messenger. When you listen to the message and make healthy changes, anxiety typically reduces or disappears.

Anxiety can come from being afraid of or obsessing on your future. When you are living in the present, anxiety has no real power. Fear of some uncertain future event or situation sparks the adrenal glands to put your system on alert. Doing this for days or even years can cause adrenal fatigue or other challenges with your body's functioning.

Anxiety can also show up as a mineral deficiency. Magnesium is a vital mineral that helps calm and soothe the body. Many people I have worked with have been experiencing stress for a period of time and may not be eating well, thus causing a mineral and vitamin deficiency. When your metabolism or your nutrition are off in some way, you will feel the results. Often you will experience anxiety or fatigue.

Empath Distress Disorder

Empath distress disorder is common with empaths who experience health challenges due to taking on other's emotions and energy. Empaths can be found in all the Essential variations. An empath has higher sensitivities to the energy in and around their world. Some empaths need help learning to discern whether what they are feeling is theirs or someone else's emotions and energy.

Empath distress disorder is a constellation of symptoms including sleep disturbance, fatigue, adrenal fatigue, appetite irregularity and other signs of becoming stressed and fatigued from taking on another person's energy. Often an empath is not initially aware of this disorder and may wonder what is wrong with them. There is nothing wrong. Your Essential system is acutely sensitive.

To help you handle this a decrease the distress disorder, set healthy boundaries, eat healthy foods that are nutrient-rich, stay hydrated and practice good discernment in matters of what you are feeling and picking up from others.

I coined this term after working with empaths who were all experiencing similar health challenges. It became clear that they were taking on the energy and emotions of others and this was crating health challenges for them. We worked on them learning to discharge energies and protect themselves because their very sensitive systems required a special way to release energy so as not to experience difficulties.

The distress leaves once you consistently learn to retain your own energy while not taking on others' energy throughout your day. This can be done. If you are taking on others' energy and emotions and having a hard time. Feel free to contact me and I will see how I can assist you. www.someonegetsme.com/contact

Depression

Depression has many forms and faces. Some respond well to medication and some do not. All depression is telling you that it is time for a change. Depression brings the message that your current level is not working for you and it is time to move forward. Sadly, many people sink further into their depression and begin to hold tightly onto the heaviness and can even get stuck there. Some people have told me that they want to feel better and more alive and still they want to remain in this heavy spot because they think it is their new normal. This is not my experience at all.

Depression is a strong and powerful messenger, telling us that there is another way to navigate your life. Depression can seem like a thin veil between you and the world or it can feel like an abyss or black hole that feels impossible to climb out of day after day.

In working with people for decades, I repeatedly hear that the depression started with some malaise or some frustration or confusion. The longer this was ignored the stronger the symptoms become. Many people said that they thought it would go away if they pushed through. In this case the person used linear problem solving to address a cyclical/spiritual crisis. Using the wrong paradigm or tool will result in ineffective results in relieving your discomfort.

Existential depression is a form of depression that is rooted in the non-physical. Often this type of depression does not respond to any medication. Many of my clients come to me reporting that they tried anti-depressants and they did not help. This is because the issue is not a mental health issue requiring medication. It is an issue requiring an energy, consciousness and paradigm adjustment.

Existential depression sounds like this: "I feel so bad and heavy. I look around and see all the problems in the world and I can see some things to do to help but I look around and there is no one who can help. Is it too late? Should I stop? Is there something wrong with me?" These existential questions actually stem from your inner desire to bring good to the world. When you perceive this is not possible or cannot be done, the only way the human form can process this heavier energy is to name it depression. The solution is to go within and make changes based on your personal calling and mission. Often it is useful to enlist the support and direction from a guide or mentor in this arena.

Remember, you are in this world and not of this world. Thus, some of your solutions may appear to be only in the physical realm. Most likely many of your solutions can be found by going within and consulting your deeper self and then bringing that information with an action plan into the physical realm.

Insomnia

Many Essentials struggle with sleep at some time or another. The idea that you will always sleep a certain amount of time every night for your entire adult life seems odd to me. We are fluid, evolving and transforming beings so it seems quite logical that how we sleep is a more organic and fluid process. When you live in a highly industrialized culture, you may be out of tune with nature and the rhythms of the seasons. We are not removed or separate from other animals and the world in general. Many people are so disconnected from the natural world that re-connecting can seem a bit foreign. As you change and evolve, it is only logical that your sleep will also shift at times.

Insomnia means that you cannot sleep even when tired. Insomnia can come from an overactive brain or overexcitability, temperature change, new environment, mental and emotional stressors that carry perceived importance.

In the winter months, I tend to sleep more than in the late spring and summer. My body naturally follows the rhythms of the seasons. For years, I resisted this and beat myself up for not being able to successfully push through and keep the same insane amount of production all year. One day I woke up as my loud inner voice said, "You are NOT A MACHINE." It was as if Spirit was yelling at me to stop pushing and to allow the rhythms of the Universe to take the lead. You are not a machine. You will experience rhythms. They are all perfect. Nothing in the natural world is late. Everything always works together if you would simply allow.

The real issue is allowing your personal flow without egoistic judgment or laziness to creep in and try to convince you that sloth is a good idea. You are in the world and not of the world. This elegant dance can, at times, seem tricky. Thus, slowing down and living from a place of inner intention is where your happiness and productive sleep live.

Often, insomnia is triggered by mental obsession (fear, guilt or worry), mineral or nutritional imbalance, adrenal fatigue and cortisol dysfunction or simply higher messages trying to come through to support and guide you that you are not paying attention to during the day.

My sleep patterns have changed over my lifetime and they also change depending upon my transformation growth and awareness. This is another area where having a community or mentor to listen to you and offer valuable lessons can be quite relieving and informative.

Whenever you awaken in the middle of the night, ask your Spirit to share any messages with you in a way you can understand. Then, quietly listen to your inner voice. Often you will have an impression or message. I do this every time I awaken. Sometimes, the message does not come immediately, but it always comes.

If you awaken and feel anxious, take several deep breaths beginning with an exhale and think the word harmony. Harmony will send the message to the brain to create harmony in your system. I also notice if I am thinking or obsessing as I awaken. If I am thinking, I note the content, write it down, then give myself permission to return to sleep with the commitment to address the content during the next day. If I am not thinking, I focus my mental attention and self-soothing. I become more attentive to my nutrition intake. I have noticed that I require additional vitamin C, omega-3s, vitamin B complex, particularly B-12, and magnesium at growth times in my cycles.

When you are having times of insomnia, do not judge yourself. Stop the belief that you MUST sleep a certain number of hours or your day will be bad. These are simply not true. When you pay attention to your body from within, you will be in touch with your natural sleep rhythms. I have times when I sleep 4 hours and am refreshed and vital all day and other times when 9-10 hours is called for as I am transforming, and my body requires more rest to grow. This is following your natural rhythms rather than the life of a machine.

Naturally, I have responsibilities and often I must comply with the expectations of my work or external time schedule. I accommodate these as best as I can with self-compassion and self-love. My biggest shift here is releasing judgment and adding self-compassion and self-love. This shift has made any external requirement more palpable and my world remains more aligned.

When you have an experience of insomnia, get curious about the message. Release the idea that you are bad, or something is wrong. Within your curiosity and increased awareness, your answers will come, and you will be assured of your next best steps.

Fatigue

Growth and transformation can take a toll on the body. As you elevate your consciousness, your body will go through changes. You are growing. As a newborn baby requires additional sleep, so too you will need more rest and sleep.

If you attempt to keep pushing and ignore your natural call for rest, you will fatigue your system. There is a delicate balance of rest, growth, transformation and fulfilling your obligations in the physical world.

Pay attention to hydrating, nourishing and resting your body as best as you can each day. Practice self-soothing. Engage in restorative actions like yoga, meditation, mindfulness, tai chi, Qi Gong and connecting with nature.

You are not a machine. You are a vital, living, breathing human being who requires love, compassion and care for optimal survival. You can release harsh expectation and judgments. You can begin to make the inner shift to a more seasonal lifestyle that honors your personal growth patterns.

The more you pay attention to your personal patterns, the less fatigue you will experience. The key is listening, paying attention and taking proper action for your highest good.

When you ignore the inner nudging or try to distract yourself. There are consequences that show up in your mental, emotional, spiritual and physical bodies. Depression, insomnia, fatigue and anxiety are not the only consequences. Cardiovascular events, kidney and liver function become affected, or become stressed and your brain can be foggy and overwhelmed to the point of freezing. If you are fatigued, pay attention to the message. You do not want to inadvertently create a major health challenge.

You are meant to live in the greater rhythmic flow of the Universe while bringing your unique vision and calling into the physical world. Whenever you are out of alignment or forcing things, there is a price to pay for your physical balance and well-being.

Now would be a great time to stop for a minute and assess your attentiveness to your transformation.

Are you honoring your physical body? Explain.

_____
_____
_____
_____

Are you growing more in tune with an alignment that serves you and others? Explain.

_____
_____
_____
_____

Are you willing to release the challenges that have brought you to a place of disharmony?

_____
_____
_____
_____

I have learned over the years that cooperating with my soul's calling is much more harmonious than trying to figure out life with my intellect leading!

Blocks to Spiritual Growth

There are obstacles to growing spiritually. When these obstacles are ignored, they cause pain and discord in all areas of your life. Freeing yourself from the blocks, known and unknown, is most important. Blocks can be long standing, generational or situational. This is not a weekend activity. You will be freeing yourself from blocks over time in many ways. Think of it as an ongoing process rather than an event.

Doubt

Doubt in you.

Many Essentials doubt if they are worthy of living the vision or calling that they are experiencing. You are worthy and able. Your calling is uniquely yours and each you are fully equipped for your calling.

Your Essential gifts are part of your equipment that is unique to you. You were born with everything you require to bring your Essential gift forward with grandeur and grace. Your personal grandeur and grace will appear differently from others. Everyone is different with their equipment and everyone is the same in that we are all fully equipped to bring our unique vision into reality. Doubt has no place in your mind or heart and thus your work is to heal old wounds, misperceptions and outdated paradigms. The time is now, and you are the one to take bold, wholehearted action using your Essential gifts.

Doubt in the Universe

I've heard the saying "Most people believe in God, yet most people do not believe God." This can be an unconscious challenge for many Essentials. *Believing in God* is a cognitive construct. *Believing God* is a more trusting and often visceral experience. There is a difference between the two. When you state a belief, you hold yet you are not sure of it at the same time, you are experiencing doubt.

I work with many talented Essentials who intellectually know their beliefs and can articulate them well. When it comes to the corresponding actions, they are often plagued with doubt. This can cause Essentials to stop their work, give in to distractions, avoid and even turn away for a time.

The best way to deal with doubt is to shed the light of truth on it and call it what it is. This alone has the ability to lower the doubt enough to allow you to make positive progress toward your vision. Doubt plagues many Essentials. Excuses and blame are signs of doubt. Shine your inner light. It will lead the way. Trust.

Worry

Worry, for me, means praying for something to go wrong. Worry is a colossal waste of time and your precious Essential resources. Worry steals today with a focus on some future uncertainty. As an Essential, your path is toward living in the present moment with your Essential gifts fully operational. This will take diligent focus and a willingness to continue to excavate old patterns and beliefs then discard and transmute whatever is outdated. Worry is outdated in the life of a transforming Essential.

When you notice worry sneaking into your thoughts or blasting into your world, take a few deep breaths, connect to your Essential gifts then bring your attention to the present moment. Remind yourself that you are on time and safe, regardless what you're thinking.

Many Essentials who have seen great visions or are in touch with a higher calling often report doubt and worry as their most formidable foes. It will take effort and focus to work toward freedom from worry. You will not perfect being worry free overnight and it is perfectly alright. Use your Essential gifts to focus your thinking, words and actions toward your awesome expression of your gifts and vision. This is one very effective way to put worry in its place.

Rather than worry, I suggest training yourself to bless when you are tempted to worry. Shift the vibration and your life also shifts. Let's shift to higher levels of blessing rather than lower levels of worry.

Fear

There are many levels of fear. Fear is a killer of inspired ideas, actions and even the way you think and operate day to day. When fears of any kind or origin are present, authentic Divine connection is hindered, clouded or cut off.

Fear is often the cause of the fight, flight, freeze response to life's events or inner dialogue. When I mention fear to my clients, they automatically think of these expressions of fear, and they are correct. As far as expressing fear, Essentials, like yourself, must learn to identify and master your fear experience. Fear is a useful emotion and can be helpful when evaluated from a higher perspective. Let's look at the function or purpose of fear.

The function or purpose, of fear is to *get ready*. It is telling you to get ready and be prepared for what is happening. When you use any fear as a call to prepare, you are now in the driver's seat for your calling and legacy. Fear gets a bad rap, and often people freeze on some level.

Try using any fears that arise to catapult you forward by being even more prepared and focusing on your next right action. The more prepared you are, the better results you will have in all life areas.

The 2 Great Saboteurs

There are 2 saboteurs lurking in your subconscious and they can cause challenges including self-sabotage. They are important to understand and not too many Essentials I work with initially understand these phenomena.

First, **unconscious resistance to change**, is one of the biggest saboteurs. I find that many of the more motivated and action-oriented Essentials who are focused on growing and transforming, struggle with unconscious resistance to change. Every person has some level of unconscious resistance to change. Even when you really want the change, there is a part of you that is underlying your adult decision-making functioning that is wanting the status quo. When you set out to change, be aware that this unconscious part of you is resisting as to keep the status quo humming right along.

Meet Sue

Sue really wants to evolve spiritually and move forward in living her life's purpose and vision. She has drive, motivation, support and a clear goal. Sue keeps sabotaging her progress. Sometimes it is distractions and sometimes she avoids focusing on her desired work. Nevertheless, Sue,

CHAPTER 12

says she wants the goal, yet she is frustrated because she thinks she is unable to get to her goal of helping more people in a more aligned manner.

Sue was willing to be curious and look within at her process of making great progress then struggling and then making progress slowly once again. When we started exploring unconscious resistance to change, Sue was initially a bit defensive, stating that she is motivated to change. I explained that it is not her motivation that is the issue. Nor is she doing anything wrong. All people have unconscious resistance to change at some point.

Unconscious resistance to change is precisely that, unconscious. I helped her see that she was not doing the non-serving actions on purpose. They were fueled by her unconscious self that wants things to always be the same. In reality, everything is always evolving and expanding, so staying the same or going back is not possible without much pain and suffering. As an Essential, you will see this in many people around you, including you. Sue began to open her mind and her curiosity. This allowed the unconscious resistance to be heard and to take the back seat instead of jumping into her life and wreaking havoc.

At times when we would speak of this, Sue would get extremely tired and almost want to sleep or nap, even in the middle of the conversation. I explained that this is her ego fighting the Truth and changes, so it is shutting down her brain. This unconscious resistance holds significant power if allowed to run the show.

Sue and I worked on being open and curious and challenging the unconscious status quo squatters. It is OK to send the old ways "home" to where they belong, you do not have to keep carrying around the old pain and resistance. I taught Sue the mantra that I was taught by my spiritual mentor: *"Thank you for serving me. I no longer need you. It is time for you to return home to serve others. Goodbye. And so, it is."* This is meant to be said firmly without negotiation. You may feel some sadness or a bit of a void in your emotions. It is important to fill the rest of your day with self-love and kindness. Fill the place where the resistance was with kindness, compassion, and love. No anger is needed. The more matter of fact and focused you remain the better your results. You may need to say good-bye several times and then refocus. It is perfectly ok to remain steadfast. Remember that if the resistance has been around a while (and I bet it has), then it may take a while to get it to leave and go home. Be clear and focused. You will succeed. You may feel a conspicuous absence of the resistance when it is gone. Good!

Second is **familiar pain**. This is a great seductress. She can get you so tangled up and distracted that you may not know why you keep creating the same painful scenarios over and over again. When pain and pleasure have bonded or fused, this powerful bond can keep you going back to painful actions and people because it is familiar and comfortable. Just because it is familiar and comfortable doesn't mean it is healthy or good for you.

Often when you are wanting to grow or make changes, you will go through a challenging time when the old way (especially if you do not want to live that way anymore) keeps trying to surface and get your attention. This is what keeps you returning to those actions and people that you say you want to be separated from at this time.

Meet Marcus

Pain and pleasure can be bonded and often they are in some situations. Marcus is a healer and he struggles with depression and self-doubt because of this pain/pleasure bond. When he experienced pain as a small boy, being spanked by his mother, he also felt the love for her and from her. Thus, love and pain were bonded. This is very common. Now, fast forward to adulthood. Marcus struggles with his own growth at times because the pain emotions break through whenever he is connecting to love in any form, relationship love and Divine Love. Marcus was experiencing a lot of frustration.

He would say to me: "Every time I am in the flow of love, I start crying and all of a sudden, I am sad." The overwhelming emotions would stop Marcus from moving into the loving space he deserved. We worked on breaking this bond which allowed Marcus the freedom to move forward without the pain interruptions.

Each person's journey is a bit different yet there are underlying qualities that are universal. Remember that your Essential journey is personal and unique. You are capable and fully equipped for your journey. In our sessions and in Marcus' homework, he began to break the bond of pain/pleasure and he is now able to experience love and pleasure without pain breaking through.

Here are the general steps we took. Again, your road will vary. These are examples that you can modify for your journey into freedom!

CHAPTER 12

Journal about the pain/pleasure incidents in 3rd person with made-up names. Create a running log of events and situations. Process with a trusted other.

Practice self-love in varied ways daily. Use mental, emotional, physical, spiritual and social avenues. Remind yourself that you are loved, and you deserve it.

Be curious. What is the pain/pleasure bond trying to say or hold in place? How can it be broken or wakened? What will need to happen to fill that space of the pain, once it is freed? Curiosity helps your mind stay open to the Divine Love that is all abounding.

Be receptive to messages and information/inspiration. Pay attention. Thank the old pain bonds for helping you along the way and the bonds are no longer needed so you can release them with love.

Be willing to take actions that move you toward your freedom.

Just as there are many blockages and challenges along your spiritual awakening path, as an Essential you are uniquely qualified and have the innate, divinely ordained ability to move beyond these challenges. As you grow and transcend, remember your lessons. This will come in handy as you work with others.

Questions to Ponder:

How does doubt impact your thoughts and words?

How does worry effect your motivation?

How are the 2 saboteurs showing up in your Essential daily life?

What are some self-love actions you take regularly?

Journal your ideas and inspirations:

Chapter 13
You are Not Alone

> *No man is an island entire of itself; every man is a piece of the continent, a part of the main.*
> *~~ John Donne*

This famous saying — "no man is an island" — describes the interconnectedness of the human experience. Nobody can make it alone. We need others to help us survive and thrive. Being interdependent is the way of the healthy and wise Essential or visionary. We're a society of healers, teachers, doctors, builders, carpenters and all else, and none of us can do everything alone all the time. The power of being interconnected is where you can really thrive as an Essential.

No one person can provide all the emotional support in any situation or relationship It's unrealistic to expect yourself to be the helper and Essential for everyone around you and you not to have ample support to keep charging your own inner batteries. No single person can do it all. When you are able to empathize and connect with the vast needs around you, it can be seducing to give your all to a project or cause. This can cause challenges if you are not first and foremost taking care of your own spiritual, emotional and physical needs.

A support system is a network of people you rely on — spiritually, emotionally, physically, mentally and socially. Having multiple peer groups works best for Essentials. Not everyone is going to understand you and your unique mission. So, create multiple peer groups and have support available in each group. If you have an intuitive idea you wish to share, call another Essential. If you need your plumbing fixed, call a friend who does plumbing for help. Each area of your life could have a group of people that fit into that area.

Have an inner circle who are your trusted confidantes. These people are there for you in the deeper ways. For some of my clients, I am in their inner circle because I understand them and will listen without bartering their information. Some of your multiple peer groups can be professionals you work with as colleagues, family and friends, even paid supports. With multiple peer groups, be willing and available to give in these groups as well. Your presence changes things so participating in both the receiving of support and the offering of support is the perfect flow for your transcendence. Both make for a healthy, wise, and satisfying life.

Having a strong support system has lasting benefits in everyday life and the long term. You will experience less stress and fatigue, your self-esteem and self-confidence will be more alive, you will experience increased peace and focus throughout the day and you will be more satisfied and joyful. Developing your support system is a great place to invest time and attention for your journey. Remember that your support system is fluid, so it will change and evolve as you make changes. Stay open and receptive, allowing the flow to be the guide.

If you don't have a healthy support system, it can be easy to put too much pressure on a single person or particular aspect of your life and this will cause stagnation, resentment and exhaustion. No one person can meet all your needs just like you cannot meet another person's needs in their entirety.

Building a support system

Building a support system can be challenging, especially if you are used to working or being on your own. If you have had any betrayal, the unhealed grief may negatively impact your growth of a support system. Building a support system can also be enlivening as you will experience deep connection with others that then support your energy, ideas and mission. Resist the idea that you are alone or have to make it alone. It is not true.

Growing your support system is an ongoing and organic process. People come and go and as you grow and transform, your needs and availability will be different. Nevertheless, paying attention to who's in your corner and who you can rely on for feedback, support and input makes your transcendent journey more amazing.

Identify areas where you desire support. Now, see who would be included in those areas. They don't have to be local. Some of my support system people are known to me only online. Yet, you definitely want support people that you have face to face, in-person engagements with from time to time as well.

As you grow and evolve, you become increasingly aware of the needs of your community and ultimately the world. Your priorities and your connection changes. In all your transformation and transcendence is the requirement for appropriate like-minded, safe support.

Humans thrive when in connection with others of like mind. Having healthy support is vital to your happiness, transformation and success.

Support can come in many forms. In my work, I am a support as a mentor and guide. My work includes education and inspiration regarding the many considerations when going through your awakening process.

Remember that connection is the correction. When you are connected with psychologically and spiritually safe people who support your journey, you thrive and are able then to turn up the brightness of your inner light. Often, just being authentically connected with others can make all the difference.

Community

Having community and being connected to others is a necessary part of being an Essential. We all need community. I suggest multiple peer groups that make up your community. Having multiple peer groups allows for more fulfillment and peace for you. Pay attention to who is in your life and what their primary role is on a daily basis. Now group the primary people into major groups. Examples of peer groups include family, gifted friends, spiritually like-minded, mentors and guides, artistic friends, vacation friends and work/school peers. Practice accessing a person from the proper peer group in order to get your needs met. You do not have to personally know everyone in your community for it to be your community. You will know them, and they will know you by vibration and connection on a soul level. Some of my communities are built around activities like sailing and quilting. By engaging in these communities, my vibration rises just by participating so these communities are equally as important as the healer, teacher, Essential communities in my life.

Remember that diversity is valued as an Essential. A diverse community means that you are poised to receive and offer more depth and connection. Imagine if everyone was the same. It would be a boring existence. Celebrate your diverse communities both local in physicality as well as spiritually. Have fun!

For example: As a mentor for visionary leaders and Essentials, I am in that peer group for many of my clients and friends. I am available to speak with and I also meet some and travel with them to support their journey more fully. No matter the setting and intensity, I offer a level of support and understanding different from a vacation friend. When my clients call me and ask me to travel with them, they are accessing that part of me that fulfills the Essential peer group. This still works for their benefit. You will want to be able to identify who is in what group for your reference. Taking a family member may not meet the same goal for my clients. By choosing the best peer group based on your need, you will yield better results and much less frustration for you and others. For both of us to benefit, I must be fully willing and available. Saying yes to travel when I do not want to do it, will stagnate both of us. Being authentic and honest are key components for an Essential who is working with others.

Being part of a community supports proper brain function and is a required aspect of a healthy life for all humans.

Who is in your community?

_____
_____
_____
_____

How do you access them?

_____
_____
_____
_____

Introverts and extroverts access support and community differently. No matter how you do it, accessing your community regularly is a must if you want to be happy and healthy. Introverts are more reserved at times, yet they have the same need to connect with others appropriately. They recharge their batteries alone and usually in quiet and solitude. Extroverts will share about connecting socially to recharge. Ambiverts can do a little of either. Know how you recharge and give yourself the permission and time to recharge so you are giving from your overflow.

CHAPTER 13

Spiritual Renewal

> *We're in need of renewal when everything feels like it's of the same importance.*
> *~~ Rob Bell*

Spiritual renewal is something to monitor and pay attention to as an Essential. It is easy to get caught up in the daily, human intensities and happenings. Be sure you are consistently recharging your batteries and paying attention to your own spiritual needs. Here are some ways to facilitate spiritual renewal.

Self-Care

Taking care of yourself is the most important thing you can do. Everyone has an opinion and suggestion. What matters most, I believe, is to listen to your personal needs and follow the self-care that works for you. It is vital that you do some things for you. If you are not caring for you then it is difficult to care for anyone else. Here are 5 simple self-care tips that you can do to get started or add to your current self-care routine.

Breathe

I know this may sound elementary or weird. The fact is that most people do not breathe enough to fully oxygenate their bodies. This yields poor metabolism, thinking and memory problems and some forms of anxiety. Think about it, when there is not enough oxygen getting to the vital organs and cells, the brain begins to send emergency signals trying to get oxygen. Thus, you yawn, or you begin to feel chest tightness and you then take a deep breath. When you sigh, that is a sign you are not breathing properly, and the brain and body are trying to self-correct. When you sigh, you are moderating some form of unresolved grief or emotional pain. It is a sign to go within and do some inner work. Take a few long, slow, deep breaths right now. Feel your body relax.

Stretch and Move Your Body

This is also a simple, yet underused, form of self-care. Take time each hour you are awake to move around. Bending and stretching your body is a great self-care tip that can be a game-changer. Sedentary lifestyles that are common can cause serious health problems and impact your emotional well-being. Being a couch potato is not healthy and it is a form of not caring for you. If you have a sedentary job, get up once and hour and stretch or move around at your desk or better yet walk the halls or go outside for 5 minutes of moving. You will find yourself refreshed and more focused on your work. There is great value in moving frequently. Your lymphatic system, which removes waste from your body, needs movement to function. Sedentary lifestyles make it more difficult to flush our systems of toxins.

Journal

Writing down your thoughts, inspirations and feelings is a healthy way to remain calm and focused on your life and goals. There are many ways to journal. You can journal in the morning in a free flow way to clear your mind for the day. This is beneficial when you have a lot on your mind, and you want to be effective or creative that day. This morning free flow writing is not meant to be re-read. It is meant to be written to release the thoughts then discarded so as not to start the mental chatter all over again.

Another journal style is to write at the end of the day, recounting the event and lessons. This is a written processing of your day. It is helpful in bringing the day to a close so you can let it go and rest.

Spiritual Lesson journals are designed specifically to document spiritual lessons and intuitions that you experience during the day. This is often sued by Essentials who have an active spiritual life.

I keep all 3 of these journals. I do not write in all them every day. I do write something every day. I write in script because it helps harmonize the brain. There is no wrong way to journal. The point is to document important ideas and events. If your life is worth living, then it is certainly worth recording in an honorable fashion.

I tell my clients to journal in the way that supports them and that they will do regularly. I believe the discipline of journaling is as important as the type of journal. I do believe in having a great pen and a nice journaling book, so I will be more inclined to follow through and actually journal. Get writing and see how much better you feel. You will also have clearer thinking and a better life focus.

People who do not journal often have a random life and they could use some added focus. Journaling really helps ease anxiety, doubts and fears.

Write your goals, dreams and ideas, this makes them a real part of your life's happiness.

Stay Hydrated

This seems so simple, yet I get a lot of push-back from my clients. It is healthy to stay hydrated. Think of it this way. The water in your body is like oil in your engine. With no oil or too little oil, the engine grinds and eventually seizes up and stops working. This is true for your body. Your body needs water to metabolize your food and get nutrients delivered to their rightful places. Water is the basic building block and is required for sustaining life. Soda is not water and caffeine and alcohol dehydrate your body.

Be sure you are drinking about half your body weight in ounces of water every day. Remember, you are hydrating today for tomorrow. There is a ton of research about what type of water to drink and what filter to use if any. My point is that having enough water is life changing. Then you can research and begin to refine your actions once you are drinking enough.

Connect

Being connected to others is vital for a long, happy life. Our entire system responds better when we are connected to others. There are 3 overarching types of connection. 1) The connection to the Universe and the Divine. Becoming more grounded in nature and the world around you are powerful for your well-being. 2) Connection to yourself is also a gamechanger. Being aware of your inner experience, emotion and desires, what you like and don't like are all important aspects of being connected. 3) Connection to others. Even introverts like me need to be connected to others if we are going to thrive and be fulfilled. All three kinds of connection work together for your welfare and transcendence. Take a minute and look around your life and support system. Who is in your corner and has your back? Who supports you even though they may not understand what you are growing through? These three types of connection are vital for your happiness and health.

Take time to connect with multiple peer groups. You are multifaceted. Thinking that one peer group will fulfill your connection is limited. You are best served by several peer groups that align with the various facets of your life. Then you can seek the corresponding peer group for any connection you want.

Remember that everything effects everything. We are all connected. We are a vital part of the natural world as we are also a vital part of the spiritual or metaphysical world. Energy cannot be destroyed so you are all alchemists because everything you think, do and say impacts all of creation.

These 5 simple self-care tips can be game changers. Do not overlook the basics in taking care of yourself. Many of my clients report that they wish they had taken better care of themselves before some problem has occurred. Take the time to practice simple self-care. It is worth your investment and then some!

Stopping Burnout

Burnout is a state of emotional, physical, and mental exhaustion that is caused by excessive and long-term stress of any kind. Burnout occurs when you feel overwhelmed, emotionally drained, and unable to meet constant demands of your job or daily life.

Burnout is a word that gets thrown around often, yet it is a real thing that causes damage to your being, especially if you are an empath or intuitive. Burnout comes in many forms and can look very different from person to person and across situations.

It is vital that you practice varied and comprehensive self-care. Burnout is a common problem among the helpers. In this manual, you are receiving many strategies and suggestions to implement to help you remain healthy, alert and enthusiastic about your Essential Gifts and your message.

Compassion Fatigue

Compassion fatigue is a weariness and inner exhaustion that comes as a result of giving and working as a healer over a period of time without fully recharging your own inner light. This is very common. When you first are aware of your Essential calling, you may be tempted to give all you've got. Stop right there. When you give everything, you've got without regard to filling your own cup, you become exhausted and disillusioned. You may even give up. This is not the goal, right?

Compassion fatigue is common among you who are serving others with your gift. In many ways, it is easy to become burned out or tired. I mean an inner weariness and fatigue that comes following doing your spiritual work without enough rest and self-rejuvenation. The average length of time many Essentials make it before experiencing a form of burnout is about 2 years. I have seen many people give up and shut down because of being so fatigued.

The key to successfully sharing your gifts over a period of time is to take frequent rests or Sabbaths. Without this discipline, you will become tired and weary. You may even give up. It is very seductive to give and give and be the shining light yet when you do not remain charged yourself, your inner battery runs down, and compassion fatigue can take you over.

Your ego can then take over and begin to lie and plant seeds of doubt, fear and worry. Compassion fatigue has then officially arrived. To remedy compassion fatigue, you must physically and spiritually rest. Rest is a very important ingredient for your light to shine and for you to truly live your calling as an Essential.

Solutions to compassion fatigue include daily quiet time and meditation. Taking time each day to reflect, connect to the Divine and to listen to your still small voice within. You know when you are connected. Listen and rest in the loving compassion of the Universe. Connect with other Essentials or healers. Have supporting dialogue and energy exchange. There is a nice synergy when you exchange energy with another of like mind. Both of you are renewed. Enlist the support of a mentor or guide to support your process, lead meditations and guide you through the rough spots. Face it, this is not an easy calling and there are rough spots,

Gratitude

For the Essential, gratitude takes on many forms and is integral in your development and transformation. Gratitude is a word that is becoming popular in our culture among those who are seeking. The gratitude that comes from the mind of someone who is grateful for a deed well done or a favor from another is good. There are deeper and more profound ways to live and breathe gratitude.

Gratitude for the Good things in your life and the Good that is all around you is a great place to start. When was the last time you slowed down enough to appreciate with an open, grateful heart, the nature that is around you? What is the temperature, the colors, sounds, smells, your inner voice, and your inner emotions? All of these are great focal points to pay attention to the gratitude you are experiencing. Knowing that there are many who are not paying attention to the little things to be grateful for each day can helps remind us to offer humble gratitude for the simple things and to support this with others.

Gratitude in the face of the undesirable things is another area of gratitude for the Essential. As an Essential, you understand that all things work together for the Good. Thus, gratitude becomes who you are rather than what you give. Is your heart bubbling over with gratitude and well wishes for the overall expansion of the Universe?

Take some time and check in with the deepest parts of you and clear out any discord and replace it with authentic gratitude. From this place, move into the rest of your day. Check within often, clear out old baggage and outdated beliefs as needed. This practice is not the time to hold any judgment. Simple clearing out the old and welcoming a consciousness of gratitude for all is what is called for as you allow your Essential gifts to emerge.

Gratitude for gratitude's sake is the third type of gratitude. This gratitude is when you are the gratitude and you experience all things working together for the good. This is a great type of gratitude to experience. This level of gratitude can take some time to authentically experience. Here, you are the gratitude, your inner essence is fully present with your Essential nature visible. The idea of giving and receiving have fallen away and you live gratitude and it emanates from your being. This powerful place brings your Essential gift into the spotlight as you live your calling and make noise!

All three types of gratitude have great value and you will find yourself moving between them in various situations and mental states. There is no wrong way to be grateful. Be aware of your gratitude styles and place where you want to enhance your gratitude inner experience. We are all growing and evolving every day. Gratitude is a spiritual principle that radiates, showing us the way.

If you become distracted or have moments of doubt or worry, this is the perfect time to fix your thinking and words on gratitude. Take a walk and take in the sights and offer gratitude for each and every sight, sound and thought. Hold gratitude in your mind no matter what for about 20 minutes. Then take some deep breaths and move back into your day, refreshed and renewed in mind and soul.

Daily Practice

> *Above all, practice being loyal to your Soul.*
> *~~ John-Roger*

Essentials are particularly sensitive to routine. Having a daily practice is amazing and can yield great safety and solace. I suggest daily practice that includes a morning and an evening routine. A routine similar to mine is below for a reference or starting place for you.

Daily practice includes eating with intention, exercise and relating to others in consistent and predictable ways that emerge from Higher Principles.

Example of a Morning Routine

Awaken and immediately focus on gratitude. Gratitude for simply being. Notice your energy and how your body, mind and soul feel. Take a few long slow deep breaths. Stretch and move gently into the day. Use water on your face or in the shower to help disconnect the energies of the night.

Take time to sit in stillness and quiet. Envision your day and the predicted events. Allow yourself to be guided regarding what to do or not do during the day. After quiet time, use your journal to document any ideas or inspirations without judgment. Release the need to figure everything out. Simply use the morning to allow, being open and receptive to incoming information.

Be sure to stay hydrated. Water is an essential element and is required for health and good spiritual connectivity. As your morning routine ends, focus your intention on being that lighthouse for others and be receptive to the opportunities that arise for you to be that beacon of light.

What is you Morning Routine?

_____
_____
_____
_____
_____
_____
_____

Example of an Evening Routine

Throughout the day you encounter many different energies. It is vital to learn to not store the energies or take them on as if they are your own. The energies around you are not yours and you taking them on causes dis-ease and physical, mental and emotional problems.

Every evening spend some quiet time as the beginning of your evening routine. Notice how you are feeling. Is there any tension, pain or resistance? It is helpful to move, shaking your body and allowing your hands and arms to tremble as you are led. Some people jump up and down, some do ecstatic dance, some shake and use their voice to release and expel any stored energies while others use fire breathing to release the day's energies. This is a vital part of your day.

After you have released the stored energies from the day, now is the time for some quiet reflection and journaling any awareness or ideas. Journal until you feel complete. Be sure you are hydrated before getting into bed.

As you get into bed, say a prayer that aligns you on your journey toward your highest good. Your prayer can be something like: "Spirit, please remove from my life the people, and things that are not serving my highest good. Bring into my life, the people and opportunities that will support and encourage my highest good. Thank you. Thank you. Thank you." Release agendas and allow the Spirit to support your journey. After the prayer you can ask the archangels to stand watch at the corners of your room. Archangel Michael, Archangel Gabriel, Archangel Uriel and Archangel Raphael can be called by name and asked to sit and protect you and your energy while you sleep. Archangels can be everywhere and with everyone simultaneously as they are not bound by form. They are unlimited and nondenominational. Part of being an Essential is to live increasingly from a conscious of unity, free from old beliefs and paradigms that are restricting.

Sleep is very important for Essentials and you want to guard it and have dedicated practice to support your rest. Many Essentials have irregular sleep patterns. It is important to honor your body and give it the rest it needs. Some nights may be less than others. Work with your emotions and energies, allowing you to rest and to be protected spiritually.

What is you evening routine?

_____
_____
_____
_____
_____
_____
_____

Build foundation

Psychological safety is vital to your success, especially when building a foundation. This means that those around you feel safe sharing and being part of your journey without the fear of ridicule or harm. You can only evolve to the level of psychological safety you have. If you are a leader, the psychological safety you offer others dictates the highest they can perform. If you are not psychologically safe, then your transcendent growth will slow down. You may experience some inner growth while not allowing the light to shine This is how many people in harmful circumstances have been able to grow spiritually and have faith in the face of torture.

Being emotionally reactive destroys the safety others around you feel. They will then shut down and the downward spiral begins. Mistakes many leaders make is to use fear and threats (passive and aggressive) to motivate. This works against your desired outcome. The lack of safety creates the workers to freeze and disengage, even though they want to please you, the leader. Emotional reactivity also slows your own development as you are spiraling in ways that are not supportive of an Essential calling.

To increase and maintain psychological safety around you, be aware. Pay attention to your demeanor and words. If you are blaming or judging, the people around you will not feel safe and things can begin to deteriorate. As an Essential, you are sensitive to feelings and energies so being aware and paying attention is vital.

When you catch yourself being judgmental or blaming take these steps.

1. Recognize your inner dialogue, attitude, words and actions.
2. Stop for a few minutes and breathe.
3. Change your thinking to focus on spiritually aligned principles.
4. Do something different – think, speak and act from integrity, truth and love
5. Hold deep compassion for yourself. Be self-forgiving.
6. Extend compassion toward others while taking the most aligned action.

Remember that safety comes before accountability. You and everyone around you need safety to be willing to risk dropping their self-guard and take authentic action.

What to do when you awaken in the middle of the night.

Waking up in the middle of the night can have different meanings and therefore paying close attention to your rhythm and experience is crucial.

Awakening between 3 and 4 am is often a sign that spiritual (higher vibration) messages are trying to come forth for you. When I awaken at this time, I always ask: *"What is the message?"* and then I listen to my inner nudges and promptings. Maybe I will "hear" a message that is in response to the prayers or intentions that I have set and asked. I always pay attention. When I am done listening, I say: *"Thank you"* and then lovingly return to sleep.

Another cause of insomnia, such as awakening after 2 hours of going to sleep, is increased cortisol levels. This most often comes from prolonged stress. Cortisol is the hormone that awakens you and for it to awaken you with only 2 hours of sleep tells you that your adrenal glands are tired

CHAPTER 13

from the stress. The remedy for this is to do stress reduction exercises and breathing. Overall life stress reduction over time will ease this challenge. Waking up after only a couple of hours can also be low blood sugar.

It is a good idea to consult with a functional medicine type professional if insomnia is a challenge. Be sure the person understands and has experience working with sensitive and transforming people. Some symptoms of transformation can mimic other challenges. Your practitioner should be skilled at this discernment.

Daily practices for Essentials vary greatly. The common and most important aspects are:

1. Breathe fully and completely
2. Remain well hydrated
3. Connect within in meditation and prayer
4. Protect your dedicated self-care time
5. Follow your daily inner guidance, trust
6. Consumer healthy, clean foods for vital energy and brain power
7. Exercise and stretch the body, and mind
8. Release the old and welcome the new

You will find your own morning and evening routines. The most important thing is that your routines fuel you properly for your journey.

Does your morning routine support your daily activities? Is there something that could be changed to make it more effective?

_____
_____
_____
_____
_____
_____
_____

Does your evening routine really cleanse the day's energies and prepare you for a restful sleep? Is there something that could be changed to make it more effective?

_____

_____

_____

_____

Be open and receptive to trying new activities and ways of being. Over time as well in certain seasons, you may feel led to change some of your routines. Follow your inner nudging and then evaluate the effectiveness. Sometimes Essentials may have an inner nudge to make a change, make the change and then realize that there is an even more effective way to implement the change. Always be open to expanding. It is perfectly okay to change your mind and try new things.

CHAPTER 13

Questions to Ponder:

Does compassion fatigue effect you? If so, how?

What are your morning and evening routines?

What do you do for self-care?

How are you stretching in beliefs, words and actions?

Journal your ideas and inspirations:

Chapter 14
Making Noise as an Essential in the Modern World

> *In the midst of movement and chaos, keep stillness inside of you.*
> *~~Deepak Chopra*

You are a leader in many regards. You may or may not identify as a leader, yet you are a leader in a vital manner. For each of us, *making noise* will look and feel different. It is this variety and that adds depth to our lives. Making noise is what Essentials are here to do. You were created to bring your unique gifts into the world in a powerful way. Remember that your gifts and your expression of those gifts is uniquely yours.

Take a moment now and take a few long, deep breaths. Listen to your inner voice and heart's desire. What is important to you? How do you see yourself bringing this into reality? Keep in mind that your inner landscape and vision is uniquely yours.

Make your notes here. DO it NOW, waiting will not serve you as your memory will change and your brain will delete some vital information that you will have to excavate later.

_____
_____
_____
_____
_____
_____
_____

These 3 things are vital as you live your Essential role in all situations. Notice that they are underlying demeanors that keep your energies and vibration elevated. Notice how you can use these to enhance your Essential gifts in the world

Take a Breath. The more you cultivate your breath, the more satisfied you will feel. Breathing is essential for life itself. Your breath is your connection within and to all of life. Air is your friend and you will not deplete the air by taking deep breaths. Check your breathing now and notice if you are breathing fully or shallower. Breathing fully decompresses your inner static and helps you open to solutions and creative ideas and pursuits. Your breath helps you remain in the moment by brining you into the moment, thus stopping the urge to be a human doer instead of a human being. BREATHE.

Bring a Smile. Your smile speaks about your inner reality and how you are bringing it into the world around you. Your smile is part of your energy currency that is a gift you share. You can be smiling energetically even when your face has a different look. I have a friend who works for Hospice and she has a smile in her energy field even when she is holding the hand of a person taking their last breath. When a smiley face is not warranted, you can have a smile in your heart.

Smiles foster creativity and invite inspired ideas to emerge from deep within your soul. Smiles shift paradigms as well as bring rapport into any situation. When you are smiling, you are creating increased vitality in your energy field. This enhances your connections and breathing as well. Emotional optimism is generated by smiles and a smiling heart. When your inner energy is elevated, you will notice a sense of amazing optimism.

How do you bring a smile into the world?

_____
_____
_____
_____

Where are the areas that you could add a smile?

_____
_____
_____
_____

Become a Yes. Having a YES! Demeanor and mentality is where your productivity live. The spirit of being open, receptive and willing to take action is vital for your Essential gifts to make noise and become obvious in the positive changes in the world. Having a YES! Demeanor does not mean that you have to do everything that comes t mind and do it right away. This creates overwhelm when you are not attentive to timing and discerning what is right for you at this time. When you are operating from a heart space you begin to have heart-centered time management which allows for a creative flow in your day to day activities.

Becoming a YES! from an egoic place creates overthinking your decisions which can cause a stagnant or static productivity in your Vision as an Essential. The YES! when coming from your heart/soul place is an open and available place of creative flow that rests assured in the perfect timing of the Universe and can create from that inner assurance.

In what areas of your life is your YES! apparent?

_____
_____
_____
_____

Where would you like to bring more of a YES!?

_____
_____
_____
_____

How do you use patience and timing to offset the tendency toward burnout?

_____
_____
_____
_____

CHAPTER 14

What is your YES! to self-care and self-development?

_____

_____

_____

_____

Living an awakened life using your Essential gifts while negotiating the modern, secular world can be tricky and interesting. There are skills to develop and understanding to reach yet what is necessary is willingness to authentically live your purpose with grace, poise, trust, and humility. To do this, you will be developing the ability to create an equilibrium that allows for times of profound stillness and also times for various types of movement. This equilibrium allows you to be in your personal flow while authentically engaging with the world around you.

It does no good to be awakening and be separate or isolated from others. Essentials are here, you are here, to bring your gifts of light and high vibration. You are not here to be taxed or taxing. Essentials learn quickly how to maintain personal energetic integrity with joy. You may be beginning your conscious unfoldment, or you may have been knowingly on the road for some time. In any case, you are on the road and you have been on this road, know it or not!

Stillness

Stillness is a great practice. You will hear many versions of stillness practice and what to do or not do. I prefer simplicity. Practice being still, both internally and externally for at least 20 minutes per day. Initially, you may take a few shorter periods of stillness that add up to about 20 minutes each day. Some people remain still for longer periods. If your day is going to be busy or hectic, take a longer stillness time or take several breaks throughout the day. In Western culture, when you are busy, you tend to ignore stillness or other quiet activities because of the idea that being busy does not allow for quiet time. Highly effective people understand that the busier you are the more stillness makes a transformative impact on your day and the outcomes. The paradox is that your intellectual mind may want to hurry which burns energy needlessly. Yet, when you take time for stillness, your brain and body operate much more effectively and efficiently, thus making your day much more satisfying and successful.

Stillness is good for you both personally and professionally. Take stillness breaks throughout your day, especially if you begin to feel hurried or stressed. You will perform better, and you will remain happier and satisfied. Sometimes, I take a few minutes in my car when I arrive at a destination to take several deep breaths and release the road tension or distracting thoughts. This helps me enter the situation with a clear mind and an open heart. I find this practice makes a huge difference in my relationship rapport and my connection to my inner guidance.

Take some time right now. Take 3 long, slow, deep breaths. Drop your shoulders, relax your jaw and breathe. Close your eyes for a minute and focus inward. Feel your heart and your breath. Notice where you feel the air moving in and out of your body. Open your eyes after a few minutes, note your experience and commence reading.

What changes did you notice in your mind and body when taking the breaths?

_____

_____

_____

_____

There are other types of meditation and ways to dial into your inner world to connect. Guided meditations can also be helpful my podcast Meditations for Visionary Leaders is a great resource and there are many more. Investigate options and use what works best for you. The important idea is that you invest in your inner stillness no matter how busy you are on the outside.

Living in the Moment

This teaching has been around for centuries. As you maintain present focus and allow yourself to be fully immersed in the eternal now, you become much more joyfully productive. In this way, you are continuously updating yourself and your approach and beliefs within the physical world. As an

Essential, your light is always expanding and shining. Do not expect things to be stagnant or remain the same because they are not linear or stagnant.

This is a time to establish and maintain a practice of being still that supports your vision and mission as an Essential. Maintaining consistent stillness and being willing to look within leads to your transformation. After all, personal and global transformation is why we are here in the first place. Being still within while there is chaos without is a developed and conditioned skill. I am sure you have met Essentials who are able to be still internally while dealing with chaos or other disappointments.

Inner stillness does not mean being walked on or passive. It is quite the opposite. When you have a consistent inner quiet and stillness, you are able to act with much more accurate focus and stronger drive. Your energy is clean, and you are on point. This is a vital skill for an Essential that lives in the everyday world with others. Inner stillness invites more effective decisions that are in alignment with your Essential variation and gifts.

Your energy and the energy of the Universe is always pulsing and vibrating. By living in the present moment, you free yourself from the stress of future or the grief of past. By living in each moment while being open and receptive, you are able to meet each moment with receptivity and a fresh vision. You become more aligned with your personal mission. Inner alignment supports you living in your Essential gift with a beautiful flow that is born of inner joy. Yes, you can have inner joy flowing even in challenging times. Living in the moment is a practice and discipline that requires daily attention.

If you have challenges with the daily practice, be gentle and compassionate with yourself. It takes some people a long time to feel connected in this deeper way. The idea is to have a focus on daily growth and transformation.

Awakened Movement

Movement and acting help you remain fully engaged in your life. This is vital for Essentials. Your movement best serves you when you are fully engaged in your daily activities without holding onto the outcomes. Essentials learn very early in the transformative process to release themselves from the bondage of expectations. The more you are consciously present with your own inner landscape and how it is interacting with the outside world, the more happiness and empowerment you will experience. Awakened movement is where your empowerment and authentic impact come together for a mighty purpose.

Proper, healthy action is required in your daily life. Moving, breathing and acting with your consciousness focused with intention is how you use movement and action to serve the greater good. Be aware and bring into consciousness your thoughts and ideas. Be willing to release attachment to outcome. This practice is life changing and takes practice. Because we live in a world of expectations and external distractions, awakened movement is a game changer as you bring your Essential gifts into the light.

Running away internally or externally does not serve the greater good and it works against your personal mission and calling. When you dissociate or distract from your iner vision and calling, you create a discord within your body, emotions and mind. This discord eventually becomes dis-ease which can be problematic for your overall health and relationships.

Examples of awakened movement include Tai Chi, QiGong, interpretive dance, yoga, stretching, nature hikes and daily activities while holding an inner intention of being conscious and present. As Ram Dass has said, *"Be here now."* By slowing down your inner world and directing your thinking and mental activity, your movement in the world becomes more intentional and awakened.

What are some ways you can employ this idea of awakened movement in your life? Write some examples than give them an authentic opportunity to elevate your inner world.

_____
_____
_____
_____
_____

Embrace Discomfort and Challenge

It is only when you come out of your comfort zone that you truly grow and transform. Experiencing discomfort with an embrace affords you the opportunity to learn the lesson, see the meaning and to transcend the limitations of your ego. Your ego is the part of you that works toward comfort and perceived safety. It will feed you information that creates the illusion that you must stay in the status quo. This is a lie.

By embracing discomfort and challenges, you position yourself to grow and transcend your current limitations in thought, word and action. Discomfort is the most essential catalyst for your personal spiritual development and progress. By resisting your *growing pains*, you slow your progress and can even create moving backwards and devolving rather than evolving.

Essentials are not meant to hang out in comfort zones of sleepwalking through life. It is time, if you haven't already, to shift your conscious actions to those that sustain your spiritual evolution, unfoldment and growth. If an idea or action does not further your personal evolution and raising your vibration, then evaluate if it is the best for you. You will most likely see where the old ideas and beliefs are holding you in a place of complacency. Eventually, this will cause you pain. Make friends with being open and receptive to your personal transformation.

It is time to focus more consistently and acutely on your personal transformation and mission as an Essential. Each of us has a personally unique mission and purpose while also being an Essential. Essentials have a greater responsibility to remain in growth and expansion while growing and evolving. Not everyone is an Essential so not everyone is best served by being in the stretch zone frequently. As an Essential, your path is marked more by growth and expansion than it is rest by definition. Make friends with growth, stretching and transformation. You will be glad you did.

No More Sleepwalking

Wake up out of the ego sleep walking trance of mediocrity and habit. When you just go through your days without really paying attention and holding higher intentions, you are essentially sleep walking. When you drive across town and cannot recall the traffic signals or your route, you are sleepwalking. When your mind checks out and you are just going about life on auto pilot, you are sleepwalking. This way of engaging with your world cheats you and everyone else of your Essential gifts coming into reality. You are here to awaken to your infinite possibilities and live them from the inside out. For this to happen, you are best served by being open and receptive to your thoughts, words, actions and environment.

When you catch yourself just going along without thought or focused intention. STOP. Take 3 deep breaths. Ask yourself: *"What is my highest and best focus?"* and then go about following that guidance. To just get by and wander through life wastes much of your amazing energy and gifts. It is time to wake up Dear One.

Become more original and inspired by allowing your imagination to expand. Then follow your bliss and allow Divine guidance to support your stepping more fully into the Truth of who you are today and every day. This keeps your life fresh and alive. The more alive and enthusiastic you are, the more you thrive and shine your inner beauty into the world. After all, this is what you are here to do as an Essential!

Be an Innovator

Use creativity in all aspects of your life. Being creative comes naturally to Essentials. Your creativity may seem blocked or elusive when you are stressed, distracted or not paying attention. This is one of the many reasons why waking up and using your creative power is so vital to your happiness and success.

You are a torchbearer and you must release the idea of being a follower or someone who copies others. You are meant to be the innovator. For me, the messages I receive may take up to 2 years before others catch on and are talking about the ideas I see. I have learned over the years to rest in the time between and know that the revelations are coming. It is great to be the innovator. You are here to push the envelope and challenge the status quo with higher, spiritual intentions and guidance rather than fear and anger.

Essentials are changemakers and being an innovator is part of the change that is being brought forth through all of us. Step up and allow your creativity to lead and be the innovator on fire with higher ideals and action plans for the betterment of all. You are here as a sort of *love worker*, bringing an elevated consciousness and new ideas to the table. Your unique noise in the Universe will certainly emanate from this place of innovation, creativity and awareness.

Authentic Communication

Be transparent and open. Allow for the Universal flow to move in and through you. Being authentic is the most valuable asset of an Essential. To be authentic requires integrity and honesty as well as consistent personal development and self-care. Take every opportunity to be your authentic and deeply vulnerable self in safe and empowering ways. Stretch your comfort zones and open up to amazing experiences. When you show up on purpose, your Essential nature is honored and your communication, verbal and non-verbal, are congruent and real.

Paying attention to the listeners language set and body language while communicating in their language style is important. Be a great listener who engages and is curious about what the speaker is sharing. Deep listening involves your mind, emotions, heart and soul. Listening with your heart to what is being said as well as what is not being said allow your inner light to shine. Your authentic listening is the vital and necessary role in authentic communication. Without deep listening, authentic communication cannot happen.

To be authentic, you must also care about yourself and others. Take good care of yourself and be assured that your authenticity and realness will shine through. When you are distracted or disconnected, everyone around you can feel this disconnection either consciously or unconsciously. Thus, focus on always improving your authenticity and be aware of how you are engaging with the world around you. This is your communication with your environment.

All Together Now

Develop the skill and ability to practice movement and stillness simultaneously. This is the way of the spiritual warrior and Essential. Stillness comes from living in your Truth with an awareness that your possibilities are infinite. Your motives come from Divine Love and are focused on the highest good for all concerned. You are moving about your environment with a flow, poise and grace. You are peaceful and calm, seeing possibilities and releasing the restricting beliefs and paradigms in which you had previously stored your memories and intentions.

To be still while moving takes great focus and a commitment to living in your authentic higher Truth. You are open to Divine guidance and the way to respond to life events.

When your movement appears suspiciously like being busy, take a few deep breaths, drop your shoulders and still your mind. Now, with intention, keep breathing slowly with a rhythm that is comfortable. Allow your breath to lead and begin to take intentional, focused action that is in alignment with your soul's purpose.

Making noise in the modern world as an Essential takes many forms. Your unique variation, personality and autobiography are all important aspects and impactors of how you will express your unique Essential variation gifts. Each one of us is a unique combination, perfectly created. We are fully equipped to do what ought to be done by us. Rest assured, if you have an inner compelling urge within you, that it is meant to be expressed in a manner that serves all concerned.

Sometime our egos or intellectual minds can miss the higher mission. This is where your awakening is vital for your success and well-being. Practice the ideas of this chapter and journal some of your inspirations, responses and as you pay close attention to your inner world.

Support others along the path as well. Essentials in all forms are not the average or common folk. You must connect with others to understand and can relate to your gifts and your life experience. By supporting others, you are supported. Thus, the circle of connection is complete, and everyone is elevated. Being selfish or refusing to support and engage with others creates isolation, loneliness and separation. This is not the goal. Let's all allow connection internally and externally to bring more harmony into our everyday lives.

Questions to Ponder:

How do you take a breath?

How are you bringing a smile?

How do you know you have become a yes?

What is your evidence that you are an innovator?

Journal your ideas and inspirations:

Chapter 15
Action Steps to Bring Your Essential Gifts into Daily Life

Here are some tangible action steps that you can keep in mind and implement which will assist and support your intentional evolution. These are meant to be a bullet point list for quick reference. Many of the ideas are expanded upon in this book.

Go where you are celebrated – not tolerated. As an Essential it is vital to surround yourself with the presence and energy of supportive others who are uplifting. If you find yourself being tolerated or tolerating a situation, it is time to take action toward a change.

Have Clarity of Vision. Vision speaks to your inner vision for your life. The clearer on the impact and outcome, the more successful and effective you become. Invest in time to always be clearer from the inside out. What are the 5 primary principles by which you live and wish to create your vision.

Freely give of yourself: your time, attention, love, company. Take the time to give the greatest gift; that of your time and attention. Instead of sending good wishes with a friend for someone, go see them yourself. Humans yearn for that personal contact. This is more crucial these days with texting, and other social media that doesn't include personal human connection. Good intentions are not the same as you actually doing the action. Of course, good boundaries are essential when considering the most effective giving scenarios and opportunities.

Listen – Really hear what is being said and choose to engage with the speaker. Learn to listen to what is not being said. This requires listening with your heart *and* your ears.

Patience - Be patient with others and allow for their process and timing. Be patient with yourself. Often, life unfolds differently than you expect yet it is still unfolding perfectly.

Open the door for your Essential Gifts to emerge. Be open and allow the real you to come out a play. Your gifts are needed and wanted. By being open, you bless you and everyone with your inner beauty and talents.

Release excuses and blame from your words and thinking. Excuses are resistance in action, and they do not belong in your awakened Essential life.

Release bitterness – Everyone is doing the best we are able in this moment and all previous moments, even when it may look differently. All resentments and bitterness are like poison running through your veins. Bitterness takes the life force from your body and illness will be your new reality. Let it go!

Keep your inner account full – Always freely offer your love and kindness. Have your love and kindness be the last thing others remember from any interaction with you. This keeps your inner resources full when you consistently are giving and serving rom your overflow. Some people refer to this as being prayed-up.

Live so you have no regrets. Be open, receptive, authentic and kind.

Put yourself in position to receive your blessings. This is important. You will have times where you will be compelled to go to an event or call someone, do it. You never know how the blessings are going to come about. Remember, you can't watch the movie without the ticket AND entering the theatre.

Demonstrate forgiveness and compassion. You and everyone else are doing the best possible in any given moment. Be that compassionate force that helps heal. Compassion and forgiveness do not take away consequence and it is not condoning bad behavior. It simply means to have compassion for the great adventure of being human,

Walk in Love – Believe the best in all. Be that beneficial influence by your energy and demeanor and if needed, use your words.

Examine self not God or the Universe when things go awry. Be willing to look within for answers. This takes courage as your ego will want to look outside of yourself. The answers are always within, always.

Use your words with intention– Speak to the answer/solution not the problem. What you speak about, you get more of in your life. Pay close attention to your words, spoken and unspoken. They are coming into reality. Choose wisely.

Plant your garden with seeds that bear the fruit you desire. Be willing to weed the garden as well as nourish the seeds as they grow into mature plants. Be sure the soil (your inner landscape) is nutrient dense.

Have Faith - Be Patient, Be Consistent

Additional actions you wish to add.

_____
_____
_____
_____
_____

There are many ways to bring your Essential gifts forward. Let your personality shine through. Never run or hide from yourself. Always choose expansion.

Appendix I
An Unsuspecting Essential Comes of Age

I did not always know that I was an Essential. In fact, in my early years, I believed just the opposite, that I was inessential. I have vivid memories of not being heard or listened to as a child. I also remember asking questions and being laughed at or told that I was special and then dismissed. Naturally, I, as children do, began to build walls to protect me from the deep and cutting pain of being rejected, dismissed and laughed at among others.

As I developed, I remember knowing things that others did not know and I had no idea how I knew these things. In fact, I thought everyone was the same and I walked around perpetually confused why I felt so different and was being treated so hurtfully most of the time. I received mixed messages from my parents. To the outsider, I was an amazing, smart and talented young girl who was going to be a doctor and help people. I was highly rewarded and praised. At home and when alone, I was often told I was a poor example of a daughter and was put down consistently. Add to this, progressive dysfunction from parents' alcohol abuse turning toward alcoholism over time. This was very confusing in my young life.

In my early adulthood, life continued to offer challenges. In college, I was often ostracized because I was a psychology major and people did not want me reading them. What I know now, is that my natural Essential gifts allow my deep listening and intuition to see deeper than many other people. I never did really fit in with my peers. I was included in many activities and I had fun on the more superficial levels. Yet, deep within was the intense feeling of separation and loneliness. I could laugh and have fun and at the end of the evening, I always felt alone and different. I still had no idea what was happening. I was focused on my career and racing sailboats. It just seemed that this is how life was. I had no other reference point.

Every man I dated would eventually say, "You can see through me so let's be friends." I had no idea what they meant; I was just being me. My self-esteem was very low due to earlier pains from being rejected and dismissed. Each time this happened, I would feel such deep wounds that I would isolate and cry until I would surface again with renewed focus on hiding my deeper inner self. I still had no idea that I was an Essential or that what I thought was wrong with me was really what was right with me. I began to ask what I did so wrong to be alone and feel so ugly.

During these years, I had no idea about spirituality, empathic ability, intuition, higher consciousness or the deeper meaning of how the Universe and people interact. I now see that my younger self was highly sensitive and was trying to navigate an insensitive world, doing the best she knew to do; often learning how to cope by the seat of her pants. I look back on these years now with such compassion for my younger self and the people I knew. I remember being so desperate for friends that I broke some of my own rules. I said things that were hurtful, having no idea that they were so hurtful, and those friends left. I held people to standards and expectations that were unrealistic and eventually blew up those relationships as well. You get the picture; my youth was challenging and confusing. I was making great grades in school and excelling in my career which helped balance the inner turmoil.

When I was about 30 years old, my life began to open, and I started seeing some of the clues I had been searching for yet were always elusive. I met people at work that shared information with me about spiritual matters. It was all so new to me. I remember being given a book entitled *Lessons in Truth* by a physician that was the Medical Director of the hospital I worked in at the time. We would sit and talk, and he would share things that I fund fascinating yet not fully comprehending. I was naive to the depth of his shares until much later. I opened the book and started reading. I put it down after about 20 pages because I had no idea what it was trying to say. I could understand the words, yet it made no real sense to me. I kept the book though because he was someone I admired.

There were many more synchronous people and events that started happening and they continue today. This time period was the beginning of my awakening and transformation. I wanted to keep learning and once my curiosity came to life, I sought any way to learn, grow and experience higher learning and consciousness. I see now that the Medical Director saw my essential gifts in me. I wonder if he could feel how closed down inside, I was or if that even mattered.

Ever since that time period I have been an active seeker and torch bearer for high ideals and consciousness within and with the people that I meet. Every new concept or understanding has helped me evolve. As I grow and learn, I notice that I am able to actively use the lessons in my work and relationships. The Universal timing is so beautiful. It is all a matter of paying attention and being aware and open minded. I am not the same person I was years ago, and I am certain that in a year or 2, I could say this again about today.

Currently, bringing more light and unity consciousness forward is most important to me. I know that as we raise our vibration and shift the paradigm to a unity consciousness, we will see the new peaceful world emerge. This will not come easily because the old ways of right/wrong and right fighting have crystalized deep within the psyche of humanity. I am consciously going deeper and deeper within to uncover old templates and echoes of times gone by in order to release them and bring in the new way of life. This deep work is not for the faint at heart. It takes focus, desire, courage, faith and trust. Yet, I am called from deep within my being to continue this journey and invite others along as well.

I don't know what will happen next. I do know that my deep focus is in awakening the Essential within each of us. Whatever your essential gift(s), bring them out. Enhance them and allow your deeper self to emerge while lovingly releasing your old ways. They are not serving you.

My life today is full of powerful synchronicities and I am learning and growing exponentially. I have a deep inner knowing that I am here to help usher in the new way. I have said Yes! The road is rocky and very challenging at times. I am not done with excavating the old from deep within my psyche. Because our minds are the last to wake up, this is taking some focus and time. I am excited for the new freedom and beauty to come.

Thank you for your presence and your desire to move forward in the right and perfect way for you. Use your Essential Gifts and allow them to take you to places you never thought possible. Then, my friend, you will know Joy, Peace and Harmony as you meet yourself again for the first time!

Appendix II

Morning and Evening Affirmations for Expansion

Standing or sitting with a straight back, say these affirmations looking at yourself in the mirror with eye contact as much as possible. These daily routines will soon be part of your daily Essential practice. You may modify them in any way that fits you best. It is the idea and consistency that matter most.

Morning Affirmation:

"I, _____, am a person of integrity who has a great attitude and is here on purpose with a mighty purpose. I am enthusiastic about my Essential mission and vision. I am grateful for my calling and I am a good steward of all the resources available to me now and in the future. My character and my conviction are aligned to serve the highest good for all concerned. My faith is solid, my hope is strong. And so it is.

Evening Affirmation:

"Thank you, _____, for being present all day and sharing your light. I know I was born to be fully alive and I am committed to this mission. As an Essential, I am grateful for my gifts and I cherish my role within my community. I am trustworthy as a steward of these precious gifts. Tonight, I am going to sleep wonderfully and dream creative, powerful dreams. I will awaken energized and ready to greet the day, allowing my gifts to emerge naturally. And so it is."

It is always good practice to have bookends for your day. These affirmations are good examples of bookends. One of my clients uses these affirmations. Use these or create your own. The message is to have consistent start and ending day routines that support your spiritual unfoldment.

Summary
A Never-ending Invitation

You may need to leave what is familiar to you as you step more fully into your Essential identity. This is common. We see it in many spiritual texts. One example is Abraham being told to leave his country and home and go where God will show him. For me, this speaks to the faith it takes to live in the light. When you live in the light, you become a blessing to all. You realize you are living the hero's journey. You must head out on your own and journey into the unfamiliar and often uncomfortable if you are going to live your higher calling.

Historically, your calling was related to your family and the family cycles. Your story, the story of an Essential, is about someone who leaves the familiar for the unknown. You might even feel compelled, as if you have no other *real* choice. You leave your familiar for a future that breaks the cycle and you head out into something that hasn't been pre-determined by your history. Back in Abraham's days, this is a new idea. Today, we you have more support to break free from old bondages. Yet, still there are ties to the older way and this is why it is so important to locate your community and become connected.

Even though many of you know you can step out on your own and might have done so to some extent, realize this remains a revolutionary idea in today's society. With many people I work with, stepping into their Essential identity requires following the stronger inner calling because the outer world around them still believes in the cycles of the old ways. Despair is rooted in the belief that things don't change and can't change moving forward so you are essentially stuck. When you are feeling despair or disappointment, go within and connect to your higher self and then follow your personal inner guidance.

Do you have a cyclical view? Do you have a view that tomorrow can be different by stepping into the unknown? You are the parent of a new type of community or idea. You are part of a community that is here to bless all the other communities of people. Your higher awareness and consciousness are part of the new. From egocentric and community centric moving toward world centric you have the choice to keep growing. You are moving forward and focusing on your expansion seems like a better idea than focusing on regressing backward.

Your ego development is a necessary part of healthy development. This is good. You work hard and learn about self-esteem. Eventually, you begin to awaken and see more is going on in the world, so you move from self and ego toward seeing a larger view of the existence. You begin to experience the lay of the land of the family and larger group or community. The customs and ways of your people are instilled in you as you grow. You have a sense of belonging, sense of serving, loyalty, sacrificing. Now you have a larger identity with something that you belong to in the greater scheme of things. Now you are realizing that there is another way to live that is bigger than yourself and it was your community. The most powerful is the one who gives their life for the well-being of the community.

Having lived through trauma, stress and disruptions, your ego development may be incomplete and as you enter adulthood you may have some work to do the clear away the old energy bondages, outdated cycles that still seem as if they are in complete control.

You realize there is life outside of your community and you begin to question how things live and move in the world. You deconstruct your awareness and construct a greater awareness which is how you elevate your consciousness and step more fully into being the Essential. You see the Truth in many communities. This sets you apart as you move from a limited to a broader stage of growth and unfoldment.

Essentials are the healers – the ones bringing our world into the light of peace, joy and hope. It is a formidable task to be an Essential as this Universal transition is unfolding. Your purpose and gifts are a unique combination to bring forth your calling with purpose. Remember, Abraham left. He stepped into more possibilities and freed himself from the old cycles. He stepped into the unknown, willingly, following directions from the Divine. It is time to move forward into a more world centric worldview to be free.

Have patience and be open to the stages of growth. Everyone is working through their stages on time. It is each person's unfolding consciousness toward awakening. Hold on to the idea that if you can wake up, anyone can wake up! Keep planting seeds and growing and invite others along the journey with you. This will help you along your path. Your frustration is because you have kept growing and maybe others are on a different trajectory. Be open and humble. The Universe is moving forward with some perceptions of stepping back at times, yet the Universe is still moving forward perfectly.

Allow yourself to open to transform and include others. You are part of the Universal flow and always are being invited to grow and move forward.

Say yes to being open. Ask the Universe to expand you and open you up to the larger Universal light.

You and your "YES" to your gifts is emerging. Your freedom lies in following your personal flow. In these, often turbulent, times of change and transformation, take good care of yourself. Keep your hope alive. Remember that your presence makes a difference and your "YES" changes things.

Being an Essential has many deep and indescribable messages and experiences. Embrace your inner light and allow it to emerge. Begin to read these things through the spiritual eye. You will then see the never-ending invitation of the universe inviting you to transcend and unfold. You always have choice. You can say *yes* to the higher calling or *no* and go back to the previous way that often causes fear and resentment.

Smile and honor who you are and your magnificent journey.

Thank you for bringing your Essential light into the world.

About Dianne A. Allen, MA

Catalyst, free thinker, ambassador, motivator, visionary are all words used to describe Dianne A. Allen, MA. Her powerful writing comes as part of her many years of assisting others with sorting out their life challenges. Dianne's education, experience and inspiration give her unique perspectives that she shares in her writing. As a Visionary Leadership Mentor, she creates exciting and diverse avenues to expanding possibilities of personal and business growth.

If you want to be free of what holds you back, Dianne has a way of offering that needed push of inspiration to get you moving for your highest good. With over 3 decades of working with personal and business development, Dianne is committed to presenting ideas and strategies in understandable and empowering ways.

Dianne has been featured on CNN, CBS, Fox and local news outlets. She has also been featured on radio and podcasts. Along with speaking at state and national conferences.

Dianne lives in Tampa Bay Florida with her canine companion Maggie. Dianne enjoys racing sailboats, quilting and writing in her leisure time. An outdoor enthusiast, Dianne can often be found on or near the water.

Additional Books by Dianne

- ***HOW TO QUIT ANYTHING IN 5 SIMPLE STEPS***
  Break the Chains that Bind You
- ***THE LONELINESS CURE***
  A Guide to Contentment
- ***7 SIMPLE STEPS TO GET BACK ON TRACK AND LIVE THE LIFE YOU ENVISION*** *(eBook only)*
- ***DAILY MEDITATIONS FOR VISIONARY LEADERS***
- ***MIDLIFE SUICIDE***
  Things to Consider (eBook only)
- ***HOPE REALIZED***
  A Daily Meditation Journal for Transformation, Healing and Growth

Dianne's Podcasts:
- *Someone Gets Me*
- *Meditations for Visionary Leaders*
- *Sailing Legends*

Dianne's Websites:
- www.someonegetsme.com
- www.visionsapplied.com
- www.msdianneallen.com

www.ingramcontent.com/pod-product-compliance
Lightning Source LLC
Chambersburg PA
CBHW030442010526
44118CB00011B/750